Walk Like a Giant,
SELL LIKE A MADMAN

Walk Like a Giant,
SELL LIKE A MADMAN

Ralph R. Roberts
with John Gallagher

HarperBusiness
A Division of HarperCollinsPublishers

HarperCollins books may be purchased for educational, business, or sales promotional use. For information please write: Special Markets Department, HarperCollins Publishers, Inc., 10 East 53rd Street, New York, NY 10022.

FIRST EDITION

Designed by Elina D. Nudelman

Library of Congress Cataloging-in-Publication Data

Roberts, Ralph R., 1958–
    Walk like a giant, sell like a madman / by Ralph R. Roberts.
      p. cm.
    Includes index.
    ISBN 0-88730-843-0
    1. Real estate business—United States—Marketing.   2. Real estate agents—United States. I. Title.
    HD1375.R594   1997
    333.33'068'8—dc21   97-8008

97 98 99 00 01 ❖/HC 10 9 8 7 6 5 4 3 2 1

I dedicate this book to my girlfriend, Kathy,
who is also my wife,
and our children,
Kolleen, Kyle, and Kaleigh,
and
to my loyal, hard-working staff
and
my customers
who help me be the best I can be

Contents

Acknowledgments

The authors would like to thank our agent, Jeff Herman; our editor at HarperCollins, David Conti; and the employees of Ralph R. Roberts Real Estate, Inc., for their help in preparation of this book, especially Joe Hafner, who read and critiqued the entire manuscript.

We would also like to thank the numerous salespeople who shared their ideas about their profession. This book would be poorer but for their help. Among those we want to thank specifically are the following:

Tom Bagby
Howard Brinton
Terry DeSelms
Allan Domb
Art Fettig
Joe Girard
James A. Good
Phil Herman
Jim McClelland
Sam Miller
Stanley Mills

Peg Ostby
Janet Parsons
Monica Reynolds
Barbara Riccio
Mike Riehl
Greg Sapp
Cindy and Paul Sper
Joe Vicari
Steve Westmark
Phyllis Wolborsky
Pat Zaby

Introduction

HELLO, I'M RALPH R. ROBERTS.

People call me America's best salesman—the Michael Jordan of real estate. As Casey Stengel used to say, you can look it up. For nine of the past eleven years, I've sold more houses than any other salesperson in the nation, and the other two years I ranked number two. As I write this chapter, I've just finished a year where I sold nearly 600 houses, or about 2 per working day. The average Realtor in America sells about 7 or 8 houses a year, and an above-average one may sell 12 or 14 houses a year. So I'm selling more than fifty times what even my above-average competitors are selling.

Time magazine recently profiled me as "America's Scariest Salesman." It's true I work harder than anybody I know at being a success. I've sold houses at my own wedding and my grandmother's funeral, but I bet Grandma would have been proud of me. I've moved twenty-three times in twenty years, because I believe you need to stay in touch with your market—and mine happens to be residential real estate. I *love* selling. So many people out there, including salespeople, hate what they do for a living. On Sunday night, they just can't stand the thought of going to work the next day. I can't stand *not* to come to work. When I go to bed and put my head on the pillow at night, I'm thinking, "Wow, tomorrow exciting things are going to happen."

My hard work has brought me a lot of success. Today, I command up to $10,000 a day in speaking fees. Salespeople pay me $2,500 a day to shadow me (i.e., to spend a day in my office observing my methods). I do about 100 radio call-in interviews a year in markets all over the country. Not bad for a working-class kid from metropolitan Detroit.

Okay, but why another book on sales? Because American business is changing, and the sales profession is changing with it. As corporations downsize, as more women enter the market, as millions leave the false security of big companies to start their own firms, millions more people are remaking themselves as entrepreneurial salespeople. My book is for them. I've always been an innovator, and my own industry—real estate—is changing, partly because of me. A salesperson today needs a lot more than a shoe shine and a smile. Salespeople need an almost magical blend of planning, innovation, street smarts, and dedication. I can show you how to get that.

By the time you finish this book, I believe you'll resolve either to be the best salesperson in your field or give up sales and go into another line of work. If you don't enjoy the sales profession, well, that's no disgrace. Just find what it is you love in life and go for it. But if you are one of those people who, like me, loves selling, then this book is for you. I can make a good salesperson better, and a great salesperson the best.

THE PLAN OF THIS BOOK

It's important to remember that I and all other super-stars—all other madmen—had to start someplace. I remember all too vividly my hard knocks and rejections and going broke. I remember being a green nineteen-year-old kid handing out my business cards in supermarkets and not really understanding why. When I help good salespeople become great, it's important to me that I don't leave behind the many beginners who are still striving to be good.

So my first two chapters will help us "check the wiring." That's where I'll talk about the basics. These two chapters will cover attitude, appearance, education, and other essentials of a sales career. They're for those of you who are starting out in the business and those of you who need a refresher course.

The next six chapters will show you how I've organized my own rise to the top. I've developed a very thorough, exacting approach to my career. It involves using assistants, technology, systems, personal marketing, and other factors. Chapters 3 through 8 will talk about my methods.

Chapters 9 through 11 deal more with the emotional background of the salesperson's life. I'm well acquainted with both the highs and the lows of that life. Overcoming adversity is a skill and an attitude we must all develop.

Just to give you an idea: As a young man in my early twenties, I lost one of the first homes I ever owned to foreclosure. At about the same time, I was fired from selling jobs not once but twice by managers who told me I had no talent and no future as a salesperson. In my late twenties, I weighed nearly 300 pounds, was suffering backaches and sore throats, and had a terrible diet. I was a workaholic who believed in laboring sixteen hours a day, seven days a week, to be successful.

Did those negatives condemn me to failure in life? You be the judge. Today, I'm happily married to my beautiful wife, Kathleen, and we have three wonderful children—Kolleen, Kyle, and Kaleigh. I spend more time with my family, yet my business is stronger than ever. I've lost over 100 pounds thanks to a healthy diet and exercise. I have more energy, happiness, and inner peace than ever. And one of those sales managers who fired me early in my career, who told me I had no talent for sales, now recruits me to speak to his salespeople about my methods of success.

What made the difference for me was attitude—a fierce determination to shape my own future rather than let past or external events shape it for me.

So let's get started, because we have a lot of ground to cover. Remember, this book is for you. If this book is

in your hands, I suspect it's because you, too, love selling as much as I do. You may be just starting out, you
may be at midpoint in your career, or you may be stuck
on a plateau and looking for a fresh start. This I
promise: Whatever level you're at in sales, this book
will polish your talent to a hard bright gleam.

1

First, Let's Check the Wiring

CAN ANYBODY TURN THEMSELVES INTO A GREAT SALESPER-
son? Let's see.

Back in the late eighties, Tom Bagby was just
another burned out, mid-career executive within the
Bell System. He had spent his entire career at the
phone company, always in some administrative job.
Aside from a short stint on the management side, he
had never worked in sales or marketing.

Tom shocked his family and friends when, in his
early forties, he told them he wanted to try his hand at
an entrepreneurial sales career. He looked at several
options, including Amway and some of the other big
network marketers. He considered many fine companies, but finally settled on SynCom, one of the new
long-distance telephone companies. Tom signs up cus-

tomers who want lower long-distance rates, but mostly he "sells opportunity." He gets other people involved as SynCom sales representatives, who in turn sign up others. With each successive rep who signs on, Tom earns benefits.

Just six or seven years after he left the ranks of middle management, Tom is perhaps the most outstanding network marketer in the nation. He has somewhere between 12,000 and 14,000 people in his network—customers and reps he has signed up, plus those in succeeding levels. Without disclosing figures, he admits to making "a fortune" each year.

SynCom has tried several times to entice him to come "inside" onto its corporate staff. Tom politely declines. He makes much more money, and gets much more satisfaction, out of being a salesperson.

"Corporate life is for the timid," he says. "The entrepreneurial life is for those bold enough to live their dreams."

I've gotten to know Tom since he became a success. I'm proud to say that many of his attitudes and techniques are the same ones I recommend to all beginners. In this chapter and the next, we'll look at some of those.

Step One: At You, Inc., You're an Entrepreneur, Not an Employee

There are probably 50 million salespeople in America. Maybe more. In a way, everyone, no matter what they do, is selling some kind of product or service. Even the president of the United States has to sell the voters on electing him! David D'Arcangelo, author of *Wealth Starts at Home*, estimates that tens of millions of Americans are starting home-based businesses based on sales. (No wonder, too. Home-based businesses cost much less to start and have a higher success rate than many traditional businesses.) In an economy based more and more on downsized, self-employed, commission-based entrepreneurial effort, everyone will be a salesperson someday. But I believe that 90 percent of all salespeople sell themselves short in their quest for success.

How? They burden themselves with the mentality of an *employee*. They go to work at a certain time, they leave at a certain time. They let the boss supply the phones and computers and marketing materials. They may even work for a fixed salary. That's totally contrary to the essence of a sales career. In sales, the more you sell, the more you make. That's the great thing about sales. It lets us—the salespeople—determine just how successful we want to be.

Many of these passive salespeople *believe* that they can sell anything. They may say, "You just get the customers in the door and I'll do the rest." You hear salespeople voice this attitude in car dealerships, clothing stores, stock brokerages, and insurance offices. It is so misguided. It is guaranteed to keep a salesperson stuck in the lower ranks of the profession.

The first step in turning yourself into a top-ranked sales professional is to think like an entrepreneur. An entrepreneur is one who sets his or her own goals—

and then finds the means to achieve them. An entrepreneur is an independent contractor, even if he or she works for a large organization like a department store or car dealership.

Being an entrepreneur means that *you* make the majority of the decisions that shape your working day. *You* create and maintain your own database of clients. *You* invest in your own technology, from a cellular phone to a computer. *You* create your own marketing materials—even if they're as simple as thank-you cards that you send to customers.

Being an entrepreneur means you set your own financial goals. These goals are independent of whatever quota your boss sets. These goals represent where you want to be in a year's time, in five years, in ten years. They can involve specific purchases you want to make, like a new house or car, or include a target date for your retirement. Your job becomes a way to fund these dreams.

This basic attitude may be the most important thing I talk about in this book. If you get nothing else right, get this right. *Think like an entrepreneur, not an employee.* What you need to realize is that you are a business all unto yourself. You're a little corporation. It's You, Inc. You can make it do whatever you want it to do. It can be as small or as large as you want. This remains true even if you work for somebody else. The true salesperson knows that he or she operates as an independent contractor—and that gives them the right to take their success to whatever level they want.

Step Two: Get All the Education You Can

The other day I was discussing with my wife the ten biggest mistakes I've made in my career, sort of mentally preparing to write this chapter. We were talking back and forth and she said, "Ralph, do you remember that agent you used to talk about when you first started out?"

Yes, I did. It was about twenty years ago, and this agent and I were both starting out in real estate. The one thing I really remember about him was that he was always taking all these courses. He was a GRI (Graduate of the Realtors Institute) before he had ever listed his first house. He was a CRS (Certified Residential Specialist) before he listed a house. He did everything, he took every class, went to every seminar. And I used to say, How crazy is that? The guy doesn't make any money. He's getting all this education—for what? What's he doing it for?

BUT I DID IT MY WAY

In contrast, I just went out and said I'm going to make the money. I don't need all the education, all I have to do is go out and work my butt off. The money will come in. I used to knock education right and left. I knew better. I was certain about that.

Today, that other agent is very successful. He's the number-five or -six agent in the metropolitan Detroit area. He's probably pulling in a quarter of a million dollars a year. What he did was to take the doctor or lawyer approach to real estate. He went out and got his education first. I, on the other hand, never even went to college. Instead, I went out and plunged right into the school of hard knocks. I was getting street smarts. I was also working like a dog to make things happen. In a sense, I was overcoming my inexperience with sheer hours worked and energy spent.

In the long run, we both became very successful agents. But how many years of hard knocks did I have to endure? Too many. Was his way better—to get all your education first? Looking back, I would say now that your education and the experience you accumulate should go hand in hand. Both should be an ongoing process. One thing I know, my way was not the way to do it, but I was too stubborn to see my mistake.

EASY IN, EASY OUT

We all know that sales is an easy profession to get into. That's why there's such a turnover. Scott McMasters, an executive with the National Auto Dealers Association (NADA), tells me that something like 50 to 75 percent of all automobile salespeople leave their dealerships each year. What an unbelievable waste! In my field, about 50 percent of the people who go into real estate sales fold within their first year in business.

I almost could have been one of them. In my youthful exuberance, my naive enthusiasm, I thought I knew it all. I had basically closed my mind to new ideas. I wasn't smart enough to realize you could never be smart enough. Looking back, I'm amazed I grew with such an attitude.

Over the years, I started realizing how important education was to my career—to the point that I became like a sponge. I couldn't get enough. In fact, when I started taking my CRS courses and my GRI classes, I saw how the knowledge I picked up could indeed make me richer as I applied it to my career. I was in the classroom devising ways to use what I was learning to make more money. (I also took an investment course, and I used what I learned to buy the office I am working in today.) I even took my GRI course over again, because another instructor was teaching it, giving me another perspective to draw knowledge from.

Scott McMasters runs NADA's new certification program for salespeople. Consisting of reading, classroom work, and a solid grounding in ethics, the program is designed to make auto salespeople more professional. The program's been underway about three years now, and already it's paying benefits. Scott tells me that turnover at auto dealerships that send their salespeople through the program has dropped to 30 percent a year. That's still high, but it's only half the national turnover rate. Think what a savings that means for everybody. The dealership doesn't have to hire and train so many new people, and the customers get a more professional, informed, and ethical salesperson to work with.

I am such a big fan of education now, because I know it helps build you into a better salesperson. I found that getting my education and increasing my knowledge gave me something very important: It allowed me to work smarter, not harder. And that should be the goal of every salesperson.

READ, READ, READ!

Your education as a salesperson is not limited to the classroom. You should read all the books you can get your hands on. There are books on service, books on time management, books on a variety of topics and subjects. You can even get books on tape if you're too busy to take the time to read. There are motivational tapes that will help you develop a better attitude and more productive mind-set. The key is to never adopt the attitude that you know it all. Then you're dead in the water and you'll lose any leadership advantage you may have.

About twelve years ago, I decided to go to the National Association of Realtors convention. I have to confess that the only reason I went was so I could write off a trip to San Francisco. I really had no intention of attending the actual convention. However, when I got there, I decided to have a quick look-see at what was going on inside the convention hall.

The strangest thing happened. I absolutely fell in love with the speakers, fell in love with the convention floor. What an amazing place to get ideas. (No matter what profession you are in, you should go to your convention and soak it all in.) At the time, I had to wonder why, from about 800,000 real estate agents in the nation, only 25,000 bothered to show up. I thought, Wow, all these great speakers, all these great ideas. Where's everybody else?

So go to seminars, take classes, go to your convention, read books, talk to other more experienced salespeople—do whatever you can do to improve yourself and your skills. My big mistake early in my career was thinking I knew it all, that I didn't need to take the time and effort to learn. How much sooner could I have improved my skills and become a top agent if I hadn't made this terrible mistake?

I also feel that this is a mistake that's not limited to beginning salespeople. To this day, I still bump into seasoned, veteran salespeople who think they can't learn anything else, that they've seen it all. It breaks my heart to see this. It could mean that these salespeople won't grow anymore. That, to me, is stagnation. That's not a good place to be. Especially in an industry—no, a world—that is changing daily with new technology that can empower us to do more things faster and better.

I guess the lesson I am trying to impart here is never stop learning. Never stop growing as a salesperson. Soak it all in like a giant sponge. You'll be better off for it. Your career will be better off for it. And your clients will be better off for it.

Step Three: You Still Need to Spend Money to Make Money

Looking back, I'd say my grandmother was one of my best mentors. She would do anything for me. All through the eighties, we would have lunch nearly once a week. She'd come to the office— my wife worked at the office at the time—and she'd take us out to lunch. I don't remember exactly what year it was, '80 or '81, when I said to her, "You know, if I had thirty thousand dollars, there's this house I could buy, and I could probably make five or ten thousand dollars profit on it." It was priced way below market, because the owners needed to sell in a hurry. They were facing foreclosure. We went on and talked about other things, but before we left lunch, she gave me the check. She said, "Pay me back when you can."

I was just twenty-three, twenty-four years old then. I probably borrowed money off my grandmother thirty or more times for different projects I'd be involved in. Now that she's no longer with us, I'm grateful that I was always able to pay her back, too. She was someone who believed in me and in what I did. She was someone who helped me find the money I needed to set myself up in business.

INVEST IN YOURSELF

All salespeople, especially those of you starting out, need a source of start-up capital. Perhaps you won't be as lucky as I was. But then, you may not need $30,000 so early in your career. You may need just a couple of thousand dollars to buy business suits to wear to your new job as a stockbroker. You may need money to buy a new laptop computer to keep track of your transactions. You may need a few hundred dollars to buy a cellular phone. Tom Bagby tells me that a new sales representative for SynCom needs to invest only $250 to get their initial batch of marketing materials.

My friend, Phyllis Wolborsky, is the top real estate agent in Raleigh, North Carolina. She sells over 200 homes a year, working just about nine months of the year. She's been the top agent in her market for almost fifteen years in a row. Phyllis and I were talking the other day, and she recalled that when she got into the industry, all she needed was an air-conditioned car to drive clients around. Today, it's much more: cellular phones, computers, assistants, and a lot of other things that we'll talk about later on. But even at the beginning of her career, she still needed that car. It took an investment to get her on the road to success.

SPEND IT TO MAKE IT

I realize that those of you starting out may have to turn to family and friends for help. That's okay. It is entirely appropriate to borrow a few thousand dollars from your parents to set yourself up in business. The amounts will seem paltry once you become a success.

But don't shrink from capitalizing your career. You've got to spend money to make money.

Step Four: Dress the Part

Not long ago, my wife and I were visiting my cousin, "Big Al" Smith, in Dallas. While there, I took a liking to the cowboy clothing I saw everywhere and I asked my cousin where I could buy some. Al replied that he needed to ask me a question first. "Ralph," he said, "do you want to look like you work on a ranch, or do you want to look like you own a ranch?" I thought about it and what the differences were, and I told him that I wanted to look like I owned a ranch. And so he directed me to the kind of store that could help me project the image I wanted for myself.

I think salespeople need to look like salespeople. You need to look like you represent your product. Obviously, if you wear a uniform in your sales job, you need to keep it neat and clean and looking professional. The world's going casual, but I couldn't disagree more with the people who tell young salespeople to dress down, be more casual, relate to your customers by being just a regular Jane or Joe.

Consider one of the really fine department stores like Nordstrom's. When customers come into that store, they can tell who the sales staff is just by looking at them. The salespeople are impeccably groomed and attentive to your needs. When people come into my office, they can tell who's working in my office. I don't necessarily think the customers and the salespeople need to look the same.

YOUR CUSTOMERS CAN TELL THE DIFFERENCE

I think that when a customer sits down with a salesperson and the salesperson is dressed professionally—has a suit and tie on—the customer feels a lot more comfortable. I've tried it different ways: I've tried to come in casual, but my customers didn't give me the same body language, the same reactions. They clearly regarded me differently, and there was a different sort of decision-making process going on.

Personally, I love shopping for clothes. I must own 200 ties. My cuff links are gold and in the shape of houses. I wear a ring that has the word "sold" on it in big letters. When I say you need to wear a business suit, that doesn't mean be boring. You can liven up your appearance with colors and patterns and accessories. Just make sure it's tasteful and within the bounds of business attire.

DRESS LIKE THE LEADER YOU ARE

Sometimes, if I'm in someone's home and the customer is wearing shorts and a casual shirt, I may take off my jacket. But I'll leave my tie knotted and my cuff links in place. I believe the customer wants us to be professional with their transaction. That includes looking the part. They'll know from my appearance that I'm serious about helping them—and that I'm good at it, too.

So I think you need to dress professionally. Salespeople are the driving force. If nothing is sold in America, this country shuts down. So we salespeople are leading the world, and we've got to look like world leaders.

Step Five: Success Leaves Big Footprints, or Find the Mentors You Need

Years ago, a motivational speaker gave me some advice that's stuck with me. He said: "If you want to be happily married, hang around with happily married people. If you want to be a good father, hang around with good fathers."

That's why I say, If you want to be a good salesperson, hang around with good salespeople. This is so true. Have you ever worked in an office or with a group of people and there was one person who complained all the time? Or maybe it was a whiner who found fault with everything? Did you notice how these people can bring down a whole office? How they negatively affect those around them? Well, the same applies to positive people, too. They can affect you in great ways.

SUCCESS STANDS OUT

Did you ever notice that successful people don't complain much? You might say, "They're successful. What do they have to complain about?" This is a case of the chicken and the egg. Which comes first? Does success generate the winning attitude, or does the winning attitude breed success?

There's no question in my mind about that. You have to want to win before you can even start to win. Success can be contagious. Most of us know what it feels like to be on a winning team. Everyone feeds off each other. They motivate each other. They share secrets, tips, and ideas. They listen to each other. They get things done together.

But remember, being a true winner is not looking down to see how many opponents you've beaten. A true winner is always looking ahead to see who he or she can catch up with or pass.

That's how it should be with your sales career. Watch and learn from the salespeople ahead of you. Use that knowledge to catch up with them. Pass them using the knowledge you got from even better salespeople. It's momentum—the momentum you gain from the combination of accumulated knowledge and a winning attitude.

MENTORS: THE ESSENTIAL INGREDIENT

I'll say it again. If you want to be a good salesperson, hang around with good salespeople. If you want to be a better salesperson, hang around with salespeople better than you. If you're happy selling 100 cars or 100 insurance policies a year, well, hang with salespeople at that same level. But if you want to learn more and bust through to the next level, then it makes perfect sense to hang around with people who are selling at a higher level. If you have a good attitude, your natural tendency is to want to rise up to their level. What a perfect motivating goal.

One of my early mistakes was not so much lacking a winning attitude. I've always had that. My mistake was not hanging around with salespeople who were better than me. Looking back, I would have started from day one. Of course, I started my sales career as a teenager. So I had the double whammy of being a wet-behind-the-ears, cocky eighteen-year-old who was going to set the world on fire. I lacked the vision to learn from those salespeople more successful than me, and more importantly, those salespeople working smarter than me.

IN THE FOOTSTEPS OF ZIG ZIGLAR

I did have idols in my youth. I listened to the motivational speakers and sales gurus all through high school. The Zig Ziglars, the Tommy Hopkinses, the Tremendous Joneses who would come to Detroit and speak. I read the books. I listened to the tapes. I even skipped school to attend their events and rallies. I didn't have enough money to get in, so I would have to go to the hall at 5:30 A.M. to sneak in.

I wouldn't hesitate to approach these incredible speakers. I was awestruck, but I would approach them after the event and ask questions or tell them how much I admired them. Zig Ziglar once asked a young Ralph Roberts, "What are you doing here, son?" I gushed out, "I got special permission to be here, sir," I lied. "Someday I'm going to be successful like you and do what you do." "I'm sure you will," he said.

His words were inspirational. What an incredible moment for me. Luckily, I wasn't afraid to approach and talk to these people. Today, I invite many speakers who come to the Detroit area to lunch. Those I'm friends with, I invite to visit with my family. I get to network with these inspirational and intelligent people. You won't believe how much you can learn.

SUCCESS LEAVES BIG FOOTPRINTS

I saw early on the value of listening and learning from my motivational idols. But at first, I failed to look to my own industry for inspiration, advice, and knowledge. That was my big mistake. Now, in hindsight, it seems too painfully obvious. Those agents who *sell* more than you may *know* more than you. Talk to them and find out what it is!

It won't be as hard as you may think to find such people. Success leaves big footprints. You ought to go to your industry conventions and listen to the speakers. When you hear speakers you like, go up and talk to them afterward. Give them your business card. Write "thank-you" letters telling them what you thought about their topics and ideas. If you meet someone who is selling of ton of products, you have an incredible opportunity to ask them questions about the business. It's like stumbling upon a gold mine of information!

DON'T BE TOO PROUD TO ASK FOR HELP

Still, there are many obstacles that stop most of us from seeking out mentor agents. Some of us are too proud. "I'd never stoop to having to ask another agent for advice." Wrong. You're not stooping down, you're working your way up. Some of us may be jealous, as in, "I'm better than that salesperson. He/she just got lucky." But sour grapes never benefited anybody. Even worse, some of us are too afraid to ask for advice, ideas, or help. Don't be afraid to approach people for advice and answers. Sure, you'll meet an occasional person who will snub you. Stay away from that person; he or she can never help you. Move on to the next person.

If you are a beginning salesperson, you can learn

from most veterans. No matter what level you are at, you can probably find someone who is producing at significantly higher levels than yourself. Seek them out. Ask them if you could spend a day with them to try to pick up some pointers. You'll be amazed at how many salespeople will say "yes." It's a big boost to anyone's ego to be admired. People love to share their knowledge with others. It makes them feel good. I can tell you from personal experience how good it feels to share ideas and knowledge with salespeople who come up to me at my speaking events.

As I said, my mistake was not hooking up with mentors in my early years. But let me tell you, I quickly made up for that mistake, soaking up as much knowledge as I could from anyone who would share it with me. Most of you know that I've put together systems that allow me to sell over 500 houses a year. Do you think I made up every one of those systems in my head? My systems are the result of twenty years of keeping my eyes open, reading, taking classes, and, just as important, watching other salespeople work.

MY SHADOW PROGRAM

I've had many superstars around the country "shadow" me and spend a day watching me work. And I've been very fortunate that they have all paid a fee to shadow me. The funny thing is, while they're learning from me, I think I learn more from them. I'm like a sponge, and I try to take everything out of them I possibly can. But to take, you have to give. You can't be afraid to share your secrets. The more you give, the more you'll get. You can only improve your industry with this mind-set. If you are approached by salespeople who want to learn from you, share with them! You'll be amazed at what you might learn. Even today, I ask other superstar salespeople if I can shadow them for a day, just to see what helpful hints I can pick up.

A MILLION QUESTIONS A YEAR

I try to give as much back to agents as I can. I speak around the country, and I answer a million real estate questions a year. Right now, besides writing this book, I'm creating tape sets and other products. Running my real estate practice and selling over 500 homes a year keeps me plenty busy. But I still have my staff block out a certain number of days a year so that salespeople can come in and shadow me. I hope you may be motivated to call my office and inquire about shadowing me. That would be great. Then I would know that this book is doing what I hoped it would do: Helping people avoid the mistakes I made years ago. And I would love to have you come down, meet the staff, and learn a ton of stuff!

Ira Hayes, a great motivational speaker and the number-one cash register salesperson in the world, would go around and speak to other cash register companies. They'd ask, "Ira, why are you here telling us your secrets? We're your competition!" And he would say, "My company can't get the people back in the office to do what I do, so they're not worried about anybody here doing it."

Unfortunately, that's incredibly true in the sales profession as a whole. There are so many opportunities to learn, yet so few go out and find them. You've read the discouraging statistics on how many salespeople drop out of their businesses every year. Some might say they don't have what it takes to succeed. I say if they have the most important component, the desire to grow and learn and improve, then they have exactly what it takes to succeed. It's all around them: Fellow salespeople who have risen to a higher level. Just go out and watch them and *learn*.

YOUR CHAPTER 1 CHECKLIST

✓ Think like an entrepreneur, not an employee. Questions to ask yourself: Am I setting my own goals? Am I preparing my own marketing materials? Am I setting my own schedule? Do I take a proactive approach to finding customers or just wait for them to walk in the door?

✓ Get all the training and education you can as early as you can.

✓ Commit yourself to lifelong learning and improvement.

✓ Take advantage of any professional certification programs in your industry. These pay benefits to you, your employer, and your customers.

✓ You'll need to invest in yourself to be a success. Start-up costs are simply a part of business.

✓ Be well-groomed and professional looking whenever you're meeting customers.

✓ Find the mentors you need. Don't be afraid to ask for advice.

2

Know Your Product, Know Yourself

IF ALL YOU DO IS READ THE FIRST TWO CHAPTERS OF MY book, you'll be a better salesperson than 90 percent of your peers. It's that simple. Most salespeople don't even fulfill the ten basic steps I'm talking about here. If you carry out these first ten steps—and *then* go on to implement the advice in the chapters that follow—you'll be a true superstar.

Want more proof? Consider Terry DeSelms, a top Realtor in Nashville. A few years ago, Terry was handling around 20 transactions a year. Not bad, but a long way from outstanding. One day, he heard about me at a sales seminar. He came up here to Detroit to shadow me for a day. *Within one year,* he had more than doubled his production to 52 transactions a year. *The following year,* he hit 100 transactions a year.

When he began to level off in the third year at 118 transactions, he knew it was time for a refresher course. I fully expect him to hit even greater heights now that he's shadowed me a second time.

So let's get back to work. Here are five more basic strategies you'll need to follow to make you a salesperson worthy of the name.

Step Six: It's Your Product, Your Territory, and You Are the Expert!

The idea that a salesperson must know his or her product sounds so basic as to almost not need saying. As my friend and mentor Bob VanGoethem puts it, "If someone is trying to sell me life insurance, I'd expect them to know the life insurance business." But you'd be surprised. Too many salespeople think that selling is about working with customers who walk in your front door. They forget that true selling starts long before that.

The sales profession is a lot like farming. We notice the results, but don't think much about the endless hours spent cultivating a sales territory—our farm—to make the results possible.

I'd like to describe for you my concept of farming a sales market. I've used the farming concept throughout my twenty-plus-year sales career. In many ways, it's the basis of my entire business. My business now encompasses a staff of nearly fifty people and a marketplace of over 60,000 households. But it all began on a much smaller basis, with just myself as an ambitious young sales agent and a territory of a few hundred homes.

I'm sure you can adapt my concept to whatever product you're selling. My goal here is to break you of that bad habit of just waiting behind your desk for customers to come to you. We need to be proactive salespeople—especially if you want to be a superstar performer like me. Dentists, stockbrokers, auto salespeople, insurance agents, home-based cosmetics salespeople, computer retailers—in fact, any salesperson I can think of—can benefit from a more systematic approach toward cultivating their farms—that is, their marketplaces.

CHOOSING MY FARM

I think I grasped from the beginning, probably by intuition, that when I chose my farm, it had to be an area that I knew and liked. I knew I'd be spending a lot of my life on my farm. I wanted it to be an area that I could drive through every single day, just to see what's new.

So when I was starting out in my business, I chose an area I knew very well. It was my hometown, the place where I grew up and had gone to high school. I think it would be impossible for me to have been so successful in an area that I didn't know as well. When my customers mention a particular street, or ask what such and such a house might sell for, I'm the expert. I know every street, and almost every house, on my farm, even though my farm now includes a market area of more than 60,000 households.

This is so important. If you're a dentist, would you live in one town and locate your office twenty-five miles away? That would be silly. You want to live near your customers. You want to be able to see them in the grocery store, park, or video store. If you're selling insurance, you've got to live near your customers, for both their convenience and yours. The same goes for network marketers of all kinds. So pick your market carefully, because you're going to be spending a lot of time there.

A BUILT-IN CUSTOMER BASE

Another advantage of picking a farm/market that I had lived in was this: I already knew a lot of people there. That gave me a head start on my personal marketing. I'll talk more about personal marketing in another chapter, but basically my goal has always been to let every person in my territory know my name and face. What better way to get a jump on that than to sell where I grew up, went to school, and had lots of friends and family?

DO SOME HOMEWORK FIRST

With so much at stake, you must choose your farm wisely. If possible, do a computer run on several potential farms before you choose one. In my case, I looked at how homes were selling in about five different neighborhoods in my hometown. I thought that if one of these areas had only four or five sales per year and another neighborhood had forty or fifty sales per year, then I wanted to work in the area of higher turnover. The more sales, the more commissions I could make—and the more customers would get to know me.

It doesn't matter if your product serves the high end or the low end of the market. Your commission from selling ten Ford Escorts may be just as great as from one Mercedes Benz, but people buy a lot more Escorts than Mercedes. Even today, I often sell homes for what other agents in more expensive neighborhoods take security deposits for. I just sell a lot more of them.

BE THERE EVERY DAY

I wanted to pick a farm that I could drive through every day. I wanted it to be convenient for me, so that I could drive through it on my way to work or home. I knew that I couldn't be successful in a marketplace if I didn't know it.

Next, I got myself a book to keep track. I used a three-ring binder. In it, I listed all the important institutions in my marketplace. That meant every church, every high school. I wrote down everything I could about those churches and schools—the names of the pastors and principals, the number of students or parishioners, what kind of self-help groups they have, what night public meetings are held, whether they offer any relocation help to families moving into that area.

I like to keep track of churches and schools for two reasons: First, they may refer business to me. Second, when I sell a home, I'm really selling the entire community, and it helps if I can say, "Mr. or Ms. Buyer, you're a Catholic or Methodist or whatever, well, here's your parish and the pastor is Father Sylvester." I'll give them the phone numbers of the church and tell them what sort of programs they offer. Or I can tell them that they'll be a short walk to the elementary school or that the school bus stops at this corner.

I also try to know every park in my marketplace, so that when I meet a family on an appointment, I can say, "Yes, your home would be within walking distance of Barbary Park."

KNOW YOUR FARM

In my early years, I walked every street in my farm. My customers had to know who I was. They had to see me as a dedicated worker. Later on, when I was really established, I could switch over to some more sophisticated marketing techniques. But in those early years, there was no substitute for getting out and meeting people.

I handed out some gift or promotional material to every household in my farm at least three times a year for the first year, and afterward once or twice a year. Holidays are a good time. My assistants and I have handed out flags on July 4th and pumpkins over Halloween.

What I'm portraying here is a system in which I've deliberately made myself the only true expert on my sales territory and the products I sell. You can do the

same. You need to know your product and its competitors thoroughly. Then you need to cultivate your market. If you're selling computers, clearly you ought to be
farming the schools in your district, because kids and
their parents buy a lot of computers. If you're selling
cars, you ought to send your personal brochure to
every graduating senior in your sales market. If you're
selling insurance or financial products, keep track of
local community college graduations or business start-
ups, because people starting careers will need financial advice.

Step Seven: Positive, Positive, Positive

Energy is something that young kids have, and people say they wish they could bottle that energy and sell
it. Well, you can. You have all kinds of negative
thoughts going in and all kinds of bad food, and the
body can only digest so much of each. Some foods you
eat slow you down, and some speed you up. The better
you eat, the better your thoughts are, the better you'll
be in sales, the better your life will be, the better everything will be.

This positive attitude is essential to your success in
sales. A lot of salespeople say, "Well, I can't sell this
because people are laid off. We have 8 percent unemployment, we have 10 percent unemployment." Well, I
always look at just the opposite. I'll say that I'm not
going to deal with the 10 percent that can't buy, I'm
going to deal with the 90 percent that can. And I've
always found that that's worked.

EVEN THE UNFORTUNATE NEED SALESPEOPLE

About ten years ago, I learned another trick: The people who are laid off might need certain products more than ever before—especially in my industry, because I sell houses. If people don't have jobs, maybe they can't afford their houses. Maybe they need to sell their houses. So I'm there to help, to give advice on that. Maybe they need to downsize. It doesn't matter what you sell. Cars are always going to get old, clothes are always going to wear out and go out of style, computer software today has the half-life of a cheeseburger. It doesn't matter what you sell or where you're selling it, there's always a market for you.

There was a cartoon in our local newspaper that showed a guy floating up to the frozen north with a cargo of refrigerators. A judge in town made a copy of it, labeled the salesman Ralph Roberts, and sent it to me with the note, "Ralph can sell anything to anybody." But anybody can. You just have to believe in your product. And don't ever blame setbacks on external forces. The only one who determines your fate is you.

BOOST YOUR INTERNAL FIRES

Here's another secret: You can improve your energy level. Even before I lost over 100 pounds, I had tremendous energy, but I've improved my energy level through my diet. I used to have the energy, but I'd have a back pain, or a sore throat, or an earache. When I started to lose the weight and eat better, I continued to be energetic, but with less pain. I believe my energy is now higher and more controlled than ever before.

You can also increase your energy by making daily deposits of positive images into your energy bank. I believe strongly in using motivational tapes and upbeat music to recharge my batteries. In my house, we've got speakers in every room so we can listen to tapes or music everywhere. I've got my own stereo system and entertainment area right in my bathroom. So when I get in there first thing in the morning, I get everything set up, my towels and all, and then I put on some music that's really got a beat. I can't make out the words in the shower, because I'm singing and dancing. I've got an oversized shower with four shower heads and two hot-water tanks, and I like to drain both those tanks. I've got my bathroom window set up so I can see my flagpole in my yard. I love this country, and I wouldn't have been able to do what I've done in any other country, so I've positioned my flagpole so I can see it from my shower, my bedroom, when I'm eating breakfast, and from about seven other spots in the house. When it's windy, it's awesome to see Old Glory snapping while listening to the music, and I think, "I'm sure glad I woke up again today."

A MIRACLE WORKER

I believe that positive energy can work miracles. Let me tell you about my friend, Stanley Mills, who happens to be the top real estate salesperson in Tennessee and one of my mentors. A few years ago, he was diagnosed with cancer. I went out and got all the people I knew to call him and fax him with good wishes. I put together a whole book of well wishes for him. A lot of us prayed and laughed with him, giving all this energy. Well, when Stanley went to California for surgery, the surgeons found that the cancer was already gone. And Stanley remains healthy today. The doctors say that maybe all that energy and praying helped. I hope it did, because I totally love the guy.

If you go lie on a bed and say, "My life's over," it may be. No matter how old you are, you have 100 percent of the rest of your life left. So if you have a sore throat, be positive about it. When Stanley had cancer, he was positive about it. Go around and say "Great!" no matter what people say. How's your wife? *"Great!"* How are your kids? *"Great!"* How's the sore throat? *"Great!"* How was the car wreck? *"Great!"* No matter what people say, say *"Great!"*

Using your positive energy to help someone or to make a sale only gives you more energy. You work hard and you lose maybe 20 percent of your energy. When you get the "yes," you get 30 percent back, so now you have maybe 110 percent of your original energy.

EMPOWERING OTHERS

Believe me, you're going to need all that positive energy to help you in your prospecting for new leads.

Prospecting is handing out your card, making calls, listening to people say "no" on the way to "yes." I've had people that I've handed my brochure tell me they're not going to sell their home for at least five years and then try to hand the card back to me. I'll tell them, "I'm still going to be in business in five years, please hang on to my card." You never know. You may hand your card out to someone in a restaurant, and later you'll walk outside and you'll see it on the ground in the parking lot. Some salespeople may get discouraged over that, but I always think, "Well, maybe a hundred people will walk by and see it and call me."

Giving positive messages to others will help you empower them. You can change the people around you and empower them to do more than they ever could on their own by just complimenting them. You can criticize someone, and they'll be 50 percent productive. You can compliment someone, and they'll be 120 percent productive.

Now, it's important that you don't confuse positive energy with a workaholic lifestyle. Energy and relaxing can and must go together. Batteries need recharging. Football players have to have a break in the game. Basketball players have to be taken out. No matter how high your energy level is, there's got to be an escape, there's got to be a break. People often say to me, "How can you work so much and never get tired?" I tell them, "That's not true. There's times I get tired. There's times I'd like to be somewhere else." I've learned over the years that if I don't want to fry myself, I need to take those breaks to replenish my energy level.

PROTECT YOUR POSITIVE ENERGY

As you strive to be the very best in your field, you may need to separate yourself from people who don't set goals or aren't positive. You can still be friends with your high school friends from down the street, but if you're always positive and setting goals and they're not, you're probably hurting all of you by maintaining close contact. Sometimes we try to push our motivation on people who don't want it. So be a little careful whom you share it with. Find people with whom you can share your goals and your positive energy.

In the same way, you need to limit the negative images you hear. I read the local pages in the papers and follow national news, but I don't believe I need to listen to every single newscast with all those car wrecks and tragedies. If you make a steady diet of bad news and negative images, there's no way it cannot affect you.

So be positive in your thoughts and in your dealings with others. Remember that: Positive, positive, positive.

Step Eight: Stop Killing Yourself to Make a Living

I used to brag that my goal was to get home from work before *Nightline* every night. In Detroit, it's on at 11:30 P.M. What a terrible goal that was. In retrospect, this obsession for my work seems like one of the biggest blunders, because it cost me the dearest of any of my mistakes. It cost me precious time with my wife and family—time I should have been investing with them instead of chasing the next deal or trying to fix the latest problem or put out the latest fire. It is time I will never, ever be able to get back.

At the time, I had no idea what I was doing to myself, my family, or my career. I loved what I was doing, and I lived for the deal. Now, looking back, I can see I was making the classic mistake that all workaholics make. I was killing myself to make a living.

FAST FOOD AND LONG HOURS

I didn't realize it back then, but I was on the road to an early grave. I was pulling into the office at 7:30 A.M. and turning out the lights and locking up at 11:00 P.M. or midnight or even 1:00 A.M. I was running around all day like a crazy man, not even stopping to take the time to eat. Lunch and dinner in those days was the drive-thru at Burger King. (Before taking a buyer to see a home, I would have to stop and throw all the burger wrappers and French fry cartons into the trunk!) Of course, with this lifestyle, I had a weight problem. I was putting all kinds of stress on my body and jeopardizing my health. It was not a good thing by any stretch of the imagination; there was no balance whatsoever.

The hard part is that I was enjoying myself. Everything centered around my work, my transactions, my listings, my closings. I like to say that I have a passion for sales, but at that time, I had an obsession. And everyone knows obsessions are never healthy. Obsessions leave a trail of victims, because there is only one focus for the person obsessed. Everything else takes second place.

TAMING THE OBSESSION

I am extremely happy to say I have tamed that obsession—or you might say that my obsession has been downgraded into a healthy passion. It took a while—and an extremely patient wife and family—but I brought it under control. Perhaps, one has to wonder, not a minute too soon. I lost over 100 pounds and am now on a strict, healthy diet and exercise program. I feel great. I take at least one day off a weekend and, most importantly, I've made a solid commitment to take my wife out every Saturday night on our "Date Night."

Okay, I had made the mistake of being a workaholic salesman who didn't have balance between my professional life and personal life. What did I learn from this? How did it help me on the road to becoming America's number-one salesperson? On the one hand, you could say my working so hard helped me build my valuable customer base that has helped me grow to a production level of over 575 homes sold in one year. And you'd be right. But could I have worked smarter instead of harder? Could I have made attempts to educate myself earlier on? Yes. As I said earlier, I should have spent time with other top agents and learned some of the systems they used to work smarter. Why smash your head against the same wall someone else has already encountered and successfully averted? One of Ralph's Rules: It's always less painful to learn from the mistakes of others than from your own.

RELAX AND EARN MONEY

How else did I benefit? Well, eventually I developed and refined the art of delegation and time management—two critical factors of my success. I don't have to tell you that salespeople are busy people. We are usually type As who have to chase our paychecks, not simply wait for them to plop in our laps like noncommission workers. Yes, it can be an exciting and lucrative way to work, but if you don't get control of your time, you will not only jeopardize your health and your relationships, you will also jeopardize your ability to be an effective salesperson—to make money.

Many superstar salespeople I have spoken with go through the same thing. They start out with an obsession—working seven days a week, twelve to sixteen hours a day. The more they work (or so they wrongly believe), the more money they can make, the more transactions they can close. Heck, I used to believe that if I wasn't in the office, I was losing business. Superstar real estate agent Phil Herman, who sells over 200 houses a year in Dayton, Ohio, said he was working seven days a week until he noticed he was losing his "edge." He was working too hard, getting too tired, and taxing himself mentally and physically. He discovered that by taking a day off, he could actually sell more real estate.

Time management can help you make the most of your hours. The goal is to maximize your time and efforts. I even brush my teeth, comb my hair, and shave in the shower. Now *that's* time management! It lets me spend a few more precious minutes with my family at the breakfast table.

IT'S NEVER TOO LATE TO LEARN

Today, I'm happy that I have delegation and time management systems in place in my office. But it wasn't always that way. Many of our best innovations are very recent. And I think some of them are the most basic things. At the time I am writing this book, I took my Franklin time management course only one year ago. That's crazy! I should have taken the course before I got into the business. That should have been a prerequisite for making things happen. Franklin planners, if used effectively and on a daily basis, will make you much more effective. By the way, when I took the Franklin seminar, my staffers, who knew me pretty well, were betting I couldn't sit still for more than an hour of the course. But I made it through the entire day, and, boy, has it improved my productivity.

What a mistake not knowing what to do with my time. People used to say, "Wow, you work 100 hours a week?!?" I'd probably say, "Yeah, I'm working 100 hours a week." But I wasn't really. I was probably getting 60 hours a week, if I was lucky, of solid work. I was wasting the other 40. That was about 2,000 hours a year of wasted time I could have spent with my family. I was at the office. I looked busy. But I wasn't being as productive as I possibly could be.

FIFTEEN MINUTES A DAY

Hopefully, you aren't making the grave mistake of working 100-hour weeks, productive or not. Whatever your working schedule, here's one of the greatest lessons I've learned: To be effective in time management, you have to spend fifteen minutes a day, whether at night before you go to bed or first thing in the morning, planning your day. I don't care what system you use or how you keep track of everything, you have to plan your day. You need to have a map to go on vacation, you need to have a set of plays to score points in a football game. You've got to have a plan, a way to know what's going to happen, what you're going to do. You've got to prioritize things. If we can't manage our own time and control buyers and sellers, how are we going to help them buy or sell their homes, cars, and boats?

Time management, delegation, and *life balance.* These are the important things I learned from my mistake of working too many hours. I see salespeople across the nation; we are a driven bunch. My advice to you is find ways to work smarter, not harder. Don't do what I did, putting in sheer hours. Find a way to work smarter, whether you take time management courses, shadow a top salesperson, or go out and hire your first assistant—or all of the above. Life's too short. Don't squander hours. Make the most of them.

Step Nine: The Grass Isn't Always Greener

It's just human nature to think that the grass is always greener on the other side. Sometimes we just get restless and want to see what's on the other side of that hill.

My friend and neighbor, auto dealer Mike Riehl, runs the biggest retail Chrysler-Plymouth dealership in the nation. He says the biggest mistake most auto sales-people make is changing dealerships every few years. Mike advises his young salespeople to establish their customer bases and then cultivate them for referrals and repeat business.

Here's a fact that may shock you: Mike tells me that *fully 70 percent of all business* done by a good car salesperson comes from either referrals or repeat business with past clients. Mike says that a top salesperson hardly even needs to talk to new customers walking through the door. He or she can handle 200 to 250 transactions a year—probably twice the average—sim-ply by cultivating a past client base. Naturally, that kind of relationship business is possible only if the salesperson stays in one place over the years.

Unfortunately, I didn't follow this good advice in my career in the late seventies and mid-eighties. I worked at so many different offices. I worked at Coldwell Banker Schweitzer. I worked at New World Real Estate. I worked at Fox Brothers Real Estate. I worked at Earl Keim—two separate offices of Earl Keim, actually. I went to Re/Max and then off to open my own office.

I can tell you from sheer experience that one place is not necessarily any better than another. I jumped from office to office for a variety of reasons. Each time I thought I would find a better situation. I have to tell you it was just more of the same.

I used to say, "It's got to be better at that office." But today I don't think there's one franchise that is necessarily better than another—a franchise that sticks out so much that you have to go there. They basically offer you the same opportunities. To me, it's more important to have longevity. It's more important to stay somewhere and make things happen.

LOSING MOMENTUM

You see, when I was hopping from company to company, I was losing momentum with each move I made. At each new office, I had to rebuild momentum. I had to get new business cards and other marketing materials. I had to let my clients know that I had moved. There was a whole new group of agents and personalities to deal with and get adjusted to, a whole new set of policies. And each office had a different mind-set, a different culture. Would I have been better off channeling that energy into building more business instead of moving around? Probably. Tom Bagby, the SynCom rep we met earlier, puts it this way: "As you jump the fence trying to get to greener pastures, sometimes you wind up in cow manure."

DON'T LEAVE, RENEGOTIATE

One of the main reasons many salespeople move is because of commission splits. If I had to do it all over again, I think instead of going to the next "best program of all time" and trying to better myself that way, I would possibly have renegotiated my commission splits. I would have renegotiated things to get what I wanted as I started becoming a high-producing agent.

Years ago, I mistakenly played the game of musical companies, trying to find something that was probably already in front of my face. The opportunity to make it big in your marketplace, office, or industry is always there in front of you, no matter where you work.

The most important resource you should be able to draw upon is not external—not the office, the other salespeople, or the equipment. It is internal. The best resource, the best tool you need to succeed, is your own will and desire. That's what it's all about. The ball, as they say, is in your court. Let's see a slam dunk!

Step Ten: Jump In!

Okay, you've got your education, your new clothes, and your Ralph Roberts motivational tapes. You've done some research on what area of sales and what geographic market appeals to you. What's next?

Simple. Jump in and get your feet wet!

At some point as you're starting out, all you can do is get experience. Pick your field and go to it. Don't worry about making mistakes. Every "no" that you hear is just a stepping stone on the way to your next "yes." Every mistake you make represents another opportunity to learn.

Back during the American Civil War, they would tell of a new regiment going up toward the front during a fierce battle. And the colonel of the regiment, when he heard the sound of the firing, asked the nearest general where he and his men should go in. "Why, go in anywhere," the fighting general cheerfully replied. "There is lovely fighting all along the line."

Take that for your motto. Whether you're selling Chevrolets or computers, refrigerators or fighter planes, women's clothing or, like me, real estate, jump in and get some experience. Good luck!

YOUR CHAPTER 2 CHECKLIST

✓ Choose your market carefully. Do some research on what segment of the market is most active. If possible, pick a geographic area that you already know well—or are willing to spend time to learn.

✓ Eliminate all the bad food and negative thoughts from your system. Respond to others in an upbeat, positive way. Protect yourself from sources of negative thoughts.

✓ Join a health club. It's good for you. Besides, you can prospect for leads while working out and write off at least part of your dues as a business expense.

✓ Don't kill yourself to make a living. Schedule time for your family and friends. Take at least one day off a week. Learn and use time management techniques. Spend fifteen minutes each day planning your activities.

✓ Don't keep jumping from job to job. A sales career pays the biggest dividends to those who dig in and cultivate their market. Constant job switches in search of better opportunities will only slow your momentum.

✓ Jump in and get some experience. There's no substitute for time spent meeting customers, working the telephones, and getting to know your product.

If You Don't Have an Assistant, You Are One

OKAY, SO WE'VE GOT YOU STARTED. BUT ONCE YOU REACH A certain plateau—and we all level off at times—how can you boost yourself to that next level? That's what we'll be exploring in this and the next several chapters.

First, though, let me demonstrate that continuous improvement is indeed possible.

My friend Janet Parsons was already a pretty fair saleswoman before she met me. A Realtor like myself, Janet had been selling homes in Springfield, Missouri, since the late seventies. By 1990, she handled thirty transactions a year and took home about $100,000 a year in commissions. Not bad. Only a handful of salespeople in Springfield did anywhere near as well as Janet.

Then she met me at a sales seminar. At first, Janet says, she didn't quite believe that I sold as many homes as I did. She was selling 30 homes a year as a top producer, and I was selling 300 by that time. Janet listened to me talk about getting to the next level—how by using assistants and technology and systems and vision, you can boost yourself like the space shuttle into a higher orbit.

And then Janet did what too few salespeople do: She went out and put the advice into practice.

"At the time," Janet says today, "I didn't have a computer, and I didn't have an assistant. I thought, What do I need those for? I'm already a top producer." But she hired her first assistant—her daughter, Trish, who had just graduated from college—and began to work on creating the systems that I use.

Today, five years later, Janet employs five assistants—all young women, including her daughter. She handles about 120 transactions a year—four times as many as she did before. Her annual salary has jumped to more than $400,000. She's now among the top-producing salespeople not only in Springfield, but in the whole Midwest. And when Howard Brinton, creator of one of the best-known series of real estate seminars in the nation, asked Janet to be a speaker on a panel of superstars, her heart leaped.

"Other than when my daughter was born," she says, "it was the proudest day of my life."

What I helped do for Janet, I can do for you. In this chapter, we'll be talking about one aspect of that continuous improvement.

EVERYONE NEEDS AT LEAST ONE

If I look back and ask, What is the main thing that's kept me alive, granted me time with my family and to travel, and still let me build a successful business, I'd have to say it's surrounding myself with a team. There comes a time in every salesperson's career when he or she says, "I'm so frustrated that I don't have time for my family, my hobbies, my church, or even time to think!" That's when you need to hire your first—or your next—assistant. That's when you need to duplicate yourself by hiring assistants who can take over the tasks that you—the salesperson—don't need to focus on.

The term "assistant" doesn't imply a menial job, either. Everyone has helpers. The chief executive officer of General Motors is, in effect, an "assistant" to the board of directors. The vice president of the United States is an "assistant" to the president; so are all the members of the cabinet. Catholics might even say that Pope John Paul II is God's assistant on Earth. No matter what industry you're in, you can have other people do some things to ease your burden.

In the previous chapter, you met my neighbor, Mike Riehl, who owns the largest Chrysler-Plymouth dealership in the nation. Mike has told me that one of his goals is to have all of his auto salespeople have assistants to handle their paperwork. Yet almost none of them do. They look at it as money coming out of their pockets. That's so short-sighted. Some of my top assistants have been with me for a decade or more. I couldn't operate my business without them. I wouldn't be able to write this book if I didn't have good people working with me to handle things while I take the time to do this.

Remember the last time you visited your dentist? You were probably greeted by a receptionist who pulled your file. Then a dental hygienist cleaned your teeth, took X rays, and asked if you had any problems. Only when all that was done did you get to see the dentist. Was that because your dentist is lazy? Of course not. It's because your dentist has learned to focus on those jobs that only he or she can do.

Sadly, too few salespeople have learned this all-important lesson.

WHY WE HESITATE

I think salespeople hesitate to hire assistants for three reasons. Number one, salespeople are control freaks; we're afraid to let things go. Second, salespeople believe that by the time they show an assistant how to do something, we could do it ourselves. Third, salespeople who do hire assistants fail to delegate the whole job, so that neither the assistant nor the salesperson is satisfied with the arrangement.

But if you haven't hired any assistants, you are one. That is, you're wasting your valuable *selling* time on all those backroom details that a good assistant can and should handle. As a top salesperson, I know I have to do certain things personally. I have to meet with my customers, I have to list houses, and I have to sell houses. But I do not have to put up lawn signs, file papers at the courthouse, answer every phone call, schedule every showing, stuff every envelope, or send out every letter.

START SMALL, GROW LARGE

I've always had assistants to help me, right from the start. In fact, I helped pioneer the concept among Realtors. Even today, close to 90 percent of all Realtors in the nation do not have any assistants. The superstars, on the other hand, usually have several.

I hired my first assistant when I was just eighteen years old. I would be working "the floor," as we say in real estate, taking my turn answering phone calls that came into the office. The duty rotates in three- or four-hour shifts. I hated the duty, hated taking calls for other agents. If a buyer or seller called looking for a salesperson to work with, I wanted to talk to them. But if a caller just wanted to leave a message for another agent, I'd tell them to call back later.

There were a lot of reasons why I didn't like taking messages. Partly, it's because I'm a terrible speller. I write sloppy, too. In about the eighth grade, I had an idea that I might be a doctor one day, and I knew that doctors were supposed to write real sloppy. So I started to practice writing illegibly, and I've never been able to break the habit. Sometimes I write so sloppy even I can't read my own handwriting.

So for all these reasons, I hated taking messages. I'd get in big trouble with the other salespeople. I was the youngest person in the office, and I guess they thought

I wasn't paying my dues. So I hired a high school student to help me after school and I probably paid her $4 an hour. Her schedule matched mine. If I had eighteen hours of floor duty one week, then she sat beside me for those eighteen hours answering phones. She gave my calls to me and took messages for everyone else. That freed me up for what I did best—working with my customers.

ADDING MORE AND MORE

Over the years, my number of assistants grew. The last year I was a salesperson for the Re/Max real estate organization—around 1990—I had as many as seven assistants. There were fifty other salespeople in that office, and none of them had even one. All those other salespeople knew that I was the top producer by far, and they all knew I had all these assistants helping me. But somehow, they never put the two together.

Today, after about twenty years in the business, I have about fifty people doing different things. My company keeps slowly mushrooming. We keep adding parts to our company that will add more to the bottom line.

Right now, I have two assistants who help me with listings. I have two who help me with buyers. We have a closing department. We have people who handle bookkeeping and public relations. We have assistants who work with people in foreclosure. In a later chapter, I'll be going into more detail on what exactly my assistants do for me. But here's the key point: All these people free me up to work with buyers and sellers.

KNOWING WHO TO HIRE

Here's a thought: You may be spending more time with your assistants than you will with your spouse. That suggests that you hire someone you can work with. It should be someone who understands your goals and shares them; someone who is looking for a career, not just a job.

My friend Monica Reynolds is the leading trainer of real estate assistants in the nation. She's published two books on the subject, including *Multiply Your Success with Real Estate Assistants*, and several audio tapes. Monica describes the ideal assistant as a person who is detail-oriented, punctual, organized, low-key, goal-oriented, and a problem solver. "Low-key" is particularly important in a busy office. An ex-teacher or ex-military person may be ideal; each has experience dealing with daily crises in a low-key, effective manner.

Maybe you noticed, but the personality of a good assistant is the direct opposite of that of a good salesperson. We salespeople are much more excitable, driven, and over the top than a good assistant should ever be. We have to be. There is a daily roller coaster that we need to stay up for. Our assistants need a much more even-tempered approach to keep us on track.

YES, WE REALLY CAN LET GO OF SOME DETAILS

I've talked with a lot of salespeople across the nation. I've spent time in dozens upon dozens of offices. What I've seen is that most salespeople hire people whom they can control 100 percent, or whom they feel completely superior to in every way. Or they hire people for whom they feel sorry and then can't fire because it's not in their personality.

We want to be nice to everyone; we want everyone to like us. But as the boss, you have some tough decisions to make.

I am very fortunate in that I have a fantastic staff. You cannot continually grow as a business or increase your production without a good staff. My listing manager, Joe Barnett, is a good place to start as an example of hiring good people. He's a retired school administrator: Who's better at people skills than a former high school principal? I mean, if he can handle a school full of rowdy teenagers, he can keep my sellers happy.

When I was hiring him, I was apprehensive, since I don't have a college degree and this man has an extensive education. He's been with me five years, and it's the best thing I've ever done. But for fifteen years prior to that, I kept putting the wrong people into that position, forcing them to fit, trying to make them something they weren't. It just didn't work out. It cost me precious time and momentum every time I had to bring in someone new. The lesson is this: You've got to hire the very best you can and find a form of compensation that will make them stay.

WHAT'S IN A NAME?

By the way, Joe illustrates another important point. You have to give your assistants titles commensurate with their responsibility. I learned that the hard way. Once, Joe went on a listing presentation for me where the customer was miffed when Joe described himself as "Ralph's assistant." The customer thought I didn't care enough about the transaction to come myself. They didn't understand that in hiring and training Joe, I was actually able to do a better job for them. Well, we lost that transaction to another salesperson. When Joe came back to the office and told me the story, I immediately gave him the title of "listing manager." That more accurately describes his level of importance in my firm.

I now give all my helpers titles that reflect the hard work they put in.

HIRE THE BEST YOU CAN GET

Today—and I admit this is fairly advanced for a salesperson—I have my own in-house CPA. (I know a lot of people will say, "I will *never* be able to afford an in-house CPA." Well, if you think *never*, you never will. But did it ever cross my mind that I would sell 300 or 400 houses?) One of the very few areas where I was smart enough, or lucky enough, not to make major mistakes early on in my career was in seeing the potential of income properties. At the time I'm writing this chapter, I own around 300 investment properties. Now, I can't handle this many without help! I have a property manager to collect the rent and my CPA to do the tax stuff for me. I also have a crew and a supervisor to go out and do the maintenance and repairs.

I've recently hired an in-house attorney. I didn't hire

an attorney because of litigation or lawsuits. There's a lot more knowledge that attorneys can bring besides litigation skills. I hired an attorney to help families facing foreclosure and work with banks on foreclosed properties. I have an attorney who can talk to them about all the legalities, like assignments and forbearance agreements. I had him get licensed in real estate, so we're protected there. I'm able to teach him what I know about real estate and use his knowledge about the law. The combination of the two has helped develop a very large profit center at Ralph R. Roberts Real Estate, Inc.—buying and selling foreclosed homes. This attorney brings a lot of knowledge to the table. But instead of being intimidated by that, I have harnessed it and turned it into a lucrative center here at my office.

Now I've taken it a step further. I've hired an in-house controller to help me direct my financial dealings and career in general. I've put together a personal advisory board comprised of people I know and respect from various backgrounds and fields. Each has his or her own expertise and specialty. Whenever I have a question or problem, I can turn to one or more of these professionals. They, in turn, can turn to me for my knowledge and expertise.

Not bad for a guy whose first assistant was a part-time teenager who answered the phones!

AVOID SNAP-JUDGMENT HIRINGS

I've learned to take my time in hiring assistants. Do not—let me repeat this—do not hire the first person who walks in your door. Take your time; a couple of weeks is not too much. Interview your top five or ten finalists a second time. Give them tests—spelling, simple math, copyediting. Have them compose a business letter on your office computer. Check their references.

Once you hire someone, have a game plan in place to train them. Teach them your trade lingo. In my business, we refer to "for sale by owner" homes as FSBOs, pronounced "fizz-bos." Your new assistant won't have a clue what most of these terms mean unless you take the time to explain the vocabulary.

The training never stops. I'm always fine-tuning things. A year ago, when I attended the National Association of Realtors annual convention in Atlanta, I took four of my assistants with me. Other salespeople thought I was being wildly extravagant to pay for so many people to come with me. But the money my assistants have made for me with the new knowledge they learned in Atlanta has long since paid for the entire trip.

PAY THEM TO KEEP THEM

I pay my people well and reward them with profit-sharing and other incentives. I'm a big believer in bonuses as a motivational tool. I want my assistants to share a sense of ownership in the business with me. The question is simple: Do you want to pay someone a low wage and replace them every two years? The momentum you lose training and retraining will by far exceed the pennies you save hiring less-experienced people.

Find good people and reward them well enough so that they will stay. Make it worthwhile to remain with you. Sometimes you can give them a reason to want to go all out for you by rewarding them with some form of partnership, vice presidency, etc. You'd be surprised at how even great performance levels can improve with the right combination of rewards and motivation.

NOW THAT YOU'VE HIRED THEM, TRUST THEM

One way to keep good people is to give them real responsibility. I let them feel that they've got a real say in what happens around here. In fact, I tell my assistants to handle any problems as best they can without coming to me. I don't even want to hear about a problem unless it's absolutely necessary, because it'll just bring me down emotionally. I'm an upbeat person, and I try to instill that in my staff, like the time I stopped at an auto supply store on my way to the office and bought spark plugs to put one on everyone's desk, just to remind us how we need to be.

Here's a special tip: When you hire new assistants, let them shadow you for a couple of days *even before* you train them. This will let them observe what you do; they'll have a better idea where their own work will fit in. They may also catch a little of your intensity. Afterward when you train them, everyone will have a better idea what their roles should be.

MY BEST ASSISTANT

Why take two weeks to hire someone, several days to train them, and spend a good amount of money paying them? Simple. The right assistant will help make you rich.

The best assistant I ever had was my wife, Kathy. When we got married, I asked Kathy to handle our investment property portfolio. As I've said, often when helping my customers buy or sell a home, I see property that can't sell right away for any number of reasons. I know that if I buy it myself, fix it up, and sell it again in a few months, I can turn a tidy profit. So I do that, and for a long time Kathy handled this side of my business. When we got married, I was buying a lot of properties (I still do), and I'd come home and hand Kathy a new file and say, "Take care of it." She'd make the payments or oversee repairs or do whatever needed to be done.

Eventually, she said she couldn't do justice to the investment portfolio and our growing family, too. It just wasn't fair to her or the kids. At the time, we had two children and seventy houses to take care of. When she gave up minding our investments, I ultimately had to hire three assistants to replace her. That's how productive she was! Kathy also hired and trained my two main assistants: my secretary, Betty Tomczak, and my administrative vice president, Jane Saigh, both of whom have been with me for eleven years.

Just think how overworked I'd have been if I'd tried to sell homes *and* handle the investment portfolio by myself, with no assistants to help. For sure, something would have snapped—probably my sanity. Hiring assistants not only made me richer, it made me healthier and happier, too.

BE KIND TO THEM, THEY'RE ONLY HUMAN

While we're talking about health and happiness, you should avoid another of the mistakes I made earlier in my career. Don't burn yourself out, of course, but don't burn out your assistants, either.

For too many years early in my career, I was doing just that. In my zeal to beat my production and income levels every year, I failed to see what I was doing to my staff. I set insane expectation levels, expecting them to keep pace, to work my hours. I expected them to share the same obsession for real estate that I had. I lost a lot of staff in those early days.

I had a young buyer's assistant for years who was outstanding. Not too many years ago, we had a good year, selling 152 homes. I sat down and projected how we were going to sell 200 homes the next year. Well, it kind of blew up in his brain and out the door he went. It pushed him over the edge. Needless to say, he quit the team and went out on his own. He's selling homes for another company—a fraction of the amount of buyers and homes he was responsible for under me, but he's still moving 50 units a year and competing directly with me. It was a painful lesson—more for having lost a great guy and incredible professional, but also for losing his production and having it come back to me as a competitor eating up some of my market share.

Luckily, one of my most valuable employees stuck it out through the tyrannical, obsessed years. Jane was one of my first assistants. She was right out of high school when she began answering phones for me. Jane has opened every department that's been created here at Ralph R. Roberts Real Estate, Inc. She's helped set the ground rules and structures for each department. What a valuable employee. We've been through so much together, I often feel like a father to her. She and her husband recently had their first child, a beautiful girl named Stephanie, and now I feel like a grandpa!

Jane will half-jokingly accuse me from time to time of having taken her late teenage years away from her. Jane survived those hectic early years because she was one of the few employees who shared my passion for sales, service excellence, and customer satisfaction. We can both look back and share some regrets, but like two soldiers who have survived in the trenches, we realize how much we've learned and how far we've come over the past eleven years. I am so glad she stuck it out, and to this day Jane plays a valuable part in my success—as do all my staff members who have stuck it out working with me all these years.

What I learned from this is that you have to be acutely aware of what your assistants' goals are. Some who work for you will have the same fire you do and are there to learn and grow. They will take whatever hours, whatever problems, and every responsibility you throw at them. Others want to work hard and contribute to your team, but are torn between their commitment to you and your team and their families. You need to help them find the right balance. Hey, you can learn from anybody. Perhaps if you are overworking yourself, you can learn balance from your staff.

YOU'RE HIRING AN EXECUTIVE ASSISTANT, NOT AN ENVELOPE STUFFER

Don't make what is probably the biggest mistake that most salespeople make with their assistants. You didn't hire them just to answer the phone or address mailings, although they may be doing those chores, too. All your assistants must be *profit centers* and *income generators* for your business. As Monica Reynolds says, "If your assistants are not an asset, they're a liability."

How to do that? One way is set up systems or departments and then delegate your staff to run them. I'll be talking more about setting up systems in a later chapter. For now, let me say a word about delegation.

All the assistants in the world won't help you if you're the kind of boss who cannot delegate. It's amazing how many salespeople in my business try to do everything themselves. They not only work with buyers and sellers—their main job—but they do all their own paperwork, call the local papers to place advertisements, and do their own taxes. It's crazy. You can easily hire assistants to do all those things, freeing you to do what you do best—work with your customers.

Take charities, for example. I'm very proud of the fact that my company gives away more than $50,000 a year to charity. We've been very fortunate that our success allows us to give to that extent. But I confess that I don't like to deal with the details myself. For one thing, it's distracting in the middle of my day. For another thing, I can never say no to anybody. So that's why I delegate our whole charitable effort to my secretary, Betty. Each year, we have a meeting to discuss what our charitable goals will be and how much we want to give away. Then she handles all the details for me. Sometimes someone will get through to me anyway, or meet me at a dinner, and I'll tell Betty the next day to send them something. She'll ask me why, since they weren't on our list, and I'll tell her I just couldn't say no to them. In other words, I don't always follow my own advice. But the more I delegate to top assistants like Betty, the better for our business.

Ralph's Rule: There has to be one person driving the bus or steering the boat. That's you—the salesperson. But there have to be other people who help make it go.

YOUR CHAPTER 3 CHECKLISTS

How to Know When to Hire an Assistant

✓ Are you frustrated?

✓ Does your family complain about not seeing you enough?

✓ Do you believe you're losing sales because of the paperwork backlog?

✓ Do you work more than sixty hours a week?

✓ Are your income and production already in the top half of your industry?

✓ Are you thinking of a career change?

If you answer "yes" to most or all of these questions, then it's time to hire your first—or next—assistant.

The Hiring, Training, and Maintaining of Assistants

✓ Take your time. Hiring an assistant is too important to rush.

✓ Interview the finalists at least twice. Test applicants on math, spelling, computers, and office routine.

✓ Find someone compatible with your energy level and goals.

✓ Have your new assistant shadow you before you train them.

✓ Train them thoroughly in your terminology, systems, computers, and goals.

✓ Delegate real responsibility to them.

✓ Reward them with good pay, bonuses, incentives, and responsibility.

✓ Keep them motivated and productive. Fire them up or fire them.

4

A Few Words About Prospecting

JAMES A. GOOD IS AMONG THE FINEST SALES TRAINERS IN the nation. His firm, James A. Good & Associates, based in Laguna Beach, California, has trained more than 100,000 salespeople, mostly stockbrokers for E. F. Hutton and other top firms. Jim's specialty is telemarketing, a field that is exploding.

When I asked Jim to explain the essence of a good telemarketer, he replied with a story that neatly makes his point. It concerns a trip Jim took when he was just a seventeen-year-old kid making his first visit to New York City.

Young Jim saw all the sights in New York—the Brooklyn Bridge, the Empire State Building, and so on. Finally, he made his way to the great theater district at Broadway and 42nd Street. He wanted to visit a world-famous deli that was known for the best sandwiches anywhere. Jim got his number and stood in line with about fifty other customers. Finally, as he neared the front of the line, the counterman called the number just preceding Jim's. No one answered. The counterman called it once more, then immediately called Jim's number.

"He didn't run out onto the sidewalk, looking for this customer who had given up his place," Jim recalls today. "He didn't waste an instant on this customer who had left. He knew that he had fifty other prospects right there in front of him, waiting for service."

The moral of the story—and of this chapter—is that prospecting for sales doesn't have to be the painful experience so many salespeople dread. There are always more prospects. Sooner or later, you'll meet that one who says "yes." Don't get hung up on the no's. Just politely thank them for their time and move on.

JUST ASK

Do you think Tom Bagby got to be one of the best network marketers in the nation by being afraid to ask people for business? Hardly. Tom tells me he asks everybody for business—friends, relatives, the dentist, everybody. Tom's philosophy is summed up in the little acronym "ASK"—Always ask, ask in Simple words, and Keep on asking.

"To let some silly fear of rejection negatively impact your financial life is lunacy," Tom says. "Courage sets you free. Remember, if you don't ask, the answer is always no!"

Jim Good calls the fear of prospecting "black-cord fever," after the black telephone cords that used to be common. Many salespeople suffer this malady. Maybe you do, too. But there's no need to despair. You can overcome it by realizing that prospecting is a numbers game. There are more than 250 million Americans. There are always more prospects.

Perhaps the difficulty some salespeople have with prospecting stems from ancient times, when a typical sales call meant traveling hundreds of miles to trade bazaars. If you didn't make a sale at the annual gathering, you went hungry. Salespeople had to grimly hang on to each prospect, asking them twenty times in twenty different ways if they'd buy something. Not so today. If someone says "no," you can immediately find a dozen more prospects. Don't get fixated on any one prospect. Just move on.

DON'T FEAR CALLING BACK

There's lots of myths about prospecting, like the one that you can only call a prospect once. What a silly idea. Jim Good once did a training seminar for E. F. Hutton brokers in Southern California. In the seminar, Jim had the stockbrokers work with a real phone list drawn from a small town. When E. F. Hutton asked Jim back to run the same seminar each month, Jim thought he'd get a different phone list drawn from a different town. Instead, Hutton provided the same list from the same small town for each meeting.

Well, the surprise was that the list just got better and better. Jim's trainees called the list once a month for three years, and it kept generating more and more business. Why? Because people were eventually ready to buy what the brokers were selling. Even if your prospect doesn't want to buy from you today, they may tomorrow. Remember what I've said before: When people hand me my brochure back and tell me they won't be in the market for a home for five years, I tell them I'll still be in business in five years and ask them to keep it.

FARM OTHER PROFESSIONALS

Now, your prospecting doesn't have to be all "cold calls," calling random names in the phone book. You can niche-market your prospecting. Remember in an earlier chapter when I described my concept of farming a territory? I try to use the same intelligent approach when prospecting.

For example, in my business, I farm between ten and thirty lawyers. When I got started with this strategy, I would call every one of them and tell them who I was and what I could do for them. Naturally, all of the buyers and sellers I deal with need some legal help. So I would mail the lawyers a monthly newsletter. I would keep reminding them that we could mutually refer business to each other. Lawyers handle all kinds of cases—probate, foreclosures, divorces—that could use the services of a good salesperson like me. Besides, lawyers know about a lot of real estate transactions in advance. In the Detroit area, I've had good success going to attorneys who work with the United Auto Workers.

I also look for sources of multiple sales. I've represented entire subdivisions, ranging in size from about fifty units to some with hundreds of homes. In your industry, whatever it is, there are probably sources of multiple sales. You'll just have to look for them.

A long time ago, I started farming five to ten insurance agents. Insurance agents know a lot about what people are buying and selling. They sell clients their home and car insurance, health insurance, and many other products. Insurance agents work on commission, just like most of us in sales. Many of my customers ask me for referrals for home insurance, and I can send a lot of business to some agents. In return, they can refer people to me.

I also farm five to ten banks. Banks know everything about the real estate in my territory, plus they have title to homes that they've foreclosed on.

What I'm portraying here is a system in which I've diversified my marketing efforts. When my work with lawyers isn't paying off, my builders may be. When my insurance agents aren't sending me referrals, perhaps my bankers are.

I also farm other salespeople outside my immediate area. About 80 percent of all people who move relocate within twenty or thirty miles of where they previously lived. But that's far enough to take them into another territory, so I farm salespeople in all the surrounding areas for business referrals. If you work for a national company, you can farm other salespeople who work in other parts of the country. You can farm smaller sales companies, offering a referral fee for business that the smaller firm is too busy to handle.

DON'T FORGET THE FOLLOW-UP

One form of prospecting that too many salespeople neglect is staying in touch with past customers. Remember, you'll get more business from past clients than from cold calling by itself. *Always* stay in touch.

There's lots of ways to do this. I'll describe more in the next chapter, but let me give you one clever idea I heard about recently. It concerns an auto dealership that urged its salespeople to cultivate their past customers for new business. So the salespeople were always sending thank-you cards and birthday cards and the like—all excellent ideas. But it was hard to distinguish their cards from all the other direct mailings from other car dealerships. One day, someone had an idea.

Whenever the dealership would sell a car, the salesperson would take the owner's manual from the car and photocopy one page out of it. Then, over the next few years, the salesperson would mail a copy of that one page to the customer on two occasions each year. The customers loved it.

What was the page? It was the one that showed customers how to reset their clocks on the dashboard. The salespeople would mail it when it was time to switch to daylight saving time in the spring and again just before we "fall back" in autumn. It was a nice little touch of service, and it reminded the customers that their salesperson was looking out for their welfare.

What a thoughtful, intelligent way to prospect for more business! I'm sure you can think of similar ways to enhance your prospecting efforts.

YOUR CHAPTER 4 CHECKLIST

✓ You can overcome fear of prospecting by remembering that it's a numbers game: There are always more prospects.

✓ Ask everyone for business.

✓ Ask simply, politely. It's a soft-sell world. Browbeating your prospects wastes both your energy and your time.

✓ It's okay to call back the same prospect several times over a period of time.

✓ Prospect among other professionals who can steer business your way.

✓ Look for clever ways to separate your prospecting from what everyone else is doing.

5

When It Comes to Personal Marketing, You *Are the Star*

I LIKE TO ASK SALESPEOPLE A SIMPLE QUESTION: CAN YOU close your eyes and visualize the president of the United States? Of course you can. So I'll continue: What does your spouse look like? What do your parents look like? What's your dog look like? What does your car look like? Can you visualize those people and things? The answer is always "yes." People either know these people and things intimately or they've seen a photograph of them—often hundreds of times.

So here's the real question: How much more would you sell if your face was that familiar to everyone in your marketplace? This is the basis of my entire marketing and promotional strategy: to make my name and face well-known to everyone in my marketplace.

It's really simple. If everyone in your area knows

what you do, you will have more business. Personal marketing—the marketing of *you* as well as the products you're selling—is essential to achieving the upper levels of success. Self-promotion is as crucial as the hiring of good assistants that I talked about in a previous chapter. If building a good staff is an "inside" strategy, one that helps you organize your office, self-promotion is an "outside" strategy. It will put your name and face before thousands of potential clients.

BUSINESS CARDS AND BALL GAMES

Now, I've never made the mistake of *not* marketing myself. From day one, I understood the power and importance of marketing me, Ralph Roberts, to the point that it's second nature. To me, it's like a game. I love selling, and one of my favorite things to sell is Ralph Roberts.

It's not because I'm stuck on myself or have a tremendous ego (although my staff might disagree with me!). It's because I am savvy enough to understand that *I* am the product. My goal is to get people excited about wanting to work with me.

Recently, an assistant and I were driving down the street and we heard a horn honking at us. A guy in the next car had my brochure with my picture on it—he was holding it in one hand and pointing at it with the other, so I don't know how he was driving—and my assistant, who was new with me, couldn't believe this. "There's a happy customer," my assistant said. And I said, *"I don't even know who he is."* Obviously, I had given him my brochure once or somebody had passed it along. But that man knew who I was, and that's what's important. The next time he needs to buy or sell real estate in my marketplace, he's going to call me.

Here's another example. Not long ago, I was in Atlanta at a convention. When the bill for dinner came, I put the credit-card slip and the tip into one of my brochures, the way I always do in restaurants. Even if someone else is paying the bill, I'll put the credit-card slip with the tip into one of my brochures. My brochures are printed in a four-color process and have several photographs of me on them. I give my brochures to waitresses, collectors at a toll booth, any-one. I probably hand out 2,000 a year, in addition to thousands more mailed out by my office.

Anyway, someone at our table said, "Ralph, you're hundreds of miles from home, why would you give out your card in Atlanta?" And everyone was laughing. But the waitress was reading my brochure and she said, "You sell homes in Detroit? My family is selling a home in metropolitan Detroit." I asked her where they lived, and it turned out to be right in my marketplace. So I called them when I got back to town and, sure enough, I got the listing and sold the house. I do not believe I would have made that sale if I hadn't been so totally committed to selling myself everywhere I go.

There are times when my zeal threatens to turn things into a three-ring circus. In 1984, the year the Detroit Tigers won the World Series, some friends and I took the train to Toronto to see the Blue Jays play. We went to three games in four days. People are still talking about this trip. I handed my business card with my photo on it (my picture has always been on my business card) to everyone on the train. At each game, I threw 1,000 business cards to the fans in the stands. I am still getting business from that train ride—more than twelve years later! I truly believe it will continue for years. I tell you, I never had so much fun marketing myself.

START SMALL, BUT START

Promoting yourself ought to come before promoting even your products or your firm. When you communicate to the general public through advertising, you should be the most dominant image on that ad. Your picture and your phone number need to be there where they can't be missed. The only way to do more business is to let people know that you're *in* business and you're going to be successful.

If you have to start small, that's okay. That's how I started. I used to advertise in church papers, the local weekly papers, and any community service newsletter that I could find. My ads in those days were neither expensive nor as sophisticated as my ads are today. But that was okay, because that was the level I was at in those days. The important thing was that I continued to work toward a higher goal. So you beginners out there should remember that there are ways to advertise that are reasonably priced. Later on, you can build up to the big stuff—PR companies, full-page ads, and that sort of thing.

Today, my personal promotional budget is about

$100,000 per year. I realize that may be a staggering figure to most salespeople, but if you start small and continue to build, you can also reach that level some day. I remember the day, say twenty years ago, when my goal was just to get one ad in a little local paper. Then I tried to get one picture in one of those freebie homes guides. Then I wanted to get my picture on my business card. I made each of these things a goal, and I achieved those and many more. But it's something that you have to build up to.

Make no mistake, as you add to your personal promotion budget, your production will increase. Even if you're just getting started, you can do something. Say you make a $2,000 commission. Try to take just $300 of that and set it aside to use toward something promotional that will work in your marketplace. As your income grows, you can increase that.

Today, I try to keep my promotional budget to around 5 percent of my earnings. Next year, I'd like to get it down to 4.5 percent, but even 1 percent on large dollars really adds up to a lot of money. To make money, you have to spend money. You have to invest. Concerts don't sell out if nobody knows about them. You're not going to make more sales if your customers don't know about you.

ZERO-BASED MARKETING

One way to get better PR cheaply is to let others pay for it. I'm serious! It's called zero-based marketing, and top salespeople use it all the time.

Remember Janet Parsons, the top Realtor in Springfield, Missouri? Janet—for business purposes—always wears smart, elegant business attire. Her photograph is on her business cards and all her promotional materials. People around town know her as the "impeccably dressed saleswoman." Other women are always asking Janet where she buys her outfits. So not long ago, Janet told the boutique where she buys her clothes that they would have to start giving her the outfits at cost. After all, Janet is referring a ton of business to them, so they can help finance Janet's wardrobe, which by now is almost purely a business expense.

In my company over the years, we've referred numerous clients to bankers, mortgage brokers, moving companies, and so forth. So when we need to produce a full-color brochure listing the homes we have for sale, I get the bankers and others that benefit from our referrals to help pay the production costs. After all, the better we do, the better they'll do.

With a little experience, you'll soon find that you can get super promotional materials at little or no cost to yourself.

AND DON'T BE BASHFUL!

I know one saleswoman who said to me once that she didn't want her picture on anything. Why not, I asked.

"I don't take a good picture," she said. "Besides, I'm ugly."

"No, you're not," I countered. "You're quite good looking, in fact."

"No, I'm not," she insisted.

"Well," I replied, trying to tease her out of it, "do you want to *surprise* your customers with that? At least let them know in advance!" And then we were both laughing about it. But seriously, I want my customers to know me in advance.

Heck, I'm even trying to get the United States government to put my picture on stamps. I haven't had real good luck with that yet, but I'm not giving up.

Since I haven't been able to get the government to put my face on stamps, I recently created my own "thank-you" stamps. They have my picture on them, and we stick them on the backs of envelopes. One of my friends—as a joke or to see what would happen— put one on an envelope where the U.S. stamp is supposed to go and mailed it to himself. It went through! So maybe I'm closer to getting my picture on a stamp than I realize.

SUPERSTAR PROMOTERS

I've always learned a great deal from other fantastic salespeople. My friend Joe Girard is famous for his books about how to sell. The Detroit-area car salesman has sold millions of copies of books like *How to Sell Anything to Anybody*. He's been translated into more than twenty languages worldwide. I met Joe years ago, and he taught me a simple but effective technique. Joe shakes hands with everybody, and everybody gets one of his business cards. Naturally, his cards have his photograph on them. Think of all the thousands upon thousands of people that Joe has shaken hands with down the years. Every one of those people has a photograph of Joe Girard. No wonder he's well-known.

Or there's Barbara Riccio of suburban Dallas, Texas, a top Realtor in her market. Each year, as a gift to her community, she throws an Easter-egg hunt that has become wildly successful. As many as 4,000 children plus their parents now attend. Barb tries to theme each hunt, so one year she brought in the California Raisins when they were popular. It's no wonder that everyone in town knows Barb's name. Think of that: A salesperson known by every person, adult or child, in her marketplace. No wonder she's a champion.

BLANKET YOUR MARKETPLACE

Okay, so now you know that you need to have your photograph on every business card and piece of correspondence that leaves your office. Who gets them? Who receives your material?

The short answer is: Everybody. You should send your promotional materials to everyone you want to be your customer. I want everyone in my marketplace to buy or sell a home with me, so that's why I send my mailings to everyone.

I'm a big believer in direct mail. Every month I send out more than 50,000 letters or brochures or other material to households in my marketplace. That's more than half a million pieces of mail a year to my sales territory—and every one of them has my photo on it at least once. If I send you a letter, at least twice in that correspondence you'll see my picture, either on the brochure or the letterhead.

Now, you may say that 50,000 pieces a month is a heck of a lot of mailings. It sure is. But I bet I'm better known in my sales territory than any other salesperson anywhere in the world. And remember, I didn't start out at that level, but worked up to it from very modest beginnings.

DON'T HIDE YOUR PHONE NUMBER

After your photograph, I believe the next most important thing on your business card or mailings is your telephone number. Not your company's main line, but your private extension. This is particularly important if you work in a big office. Why should you advertise your company's number if calls can go to any one of thirty other salespeople besides you?

If your company brochures list only the main number, then you can do some personal marketing to let people know your private line. If all your marketing material is generated by your company and doesn't mention you, then when you go on sales calls, you can hand out some personal marketing material. That will make you look that much better than your competition.

MAIL AND MORE MAIL

Besides general mass mailings, I send appeals to specific groups. I mail to every expired home listing in my marketplace. An expired listing is one in which

another Realtor couldn't sell a home within the contract time. If the other agent couldn't do the job for the
sellers, I can.

I also mail my brochures to every "for sale by
owner" in my marketplace. And I mail to every household facing foreclosure. I've even set up a separate
division in my company to work with distressed
homeowners. I'll try to find a way to let them get out
from under their foreclosure while still maintaining
residence in their home or at least in another home.

I also work with couples going through divorces.
These couples are going through an extremely painful,
often bitter process. Questions of who gets the home or
how they sell it and divide the proceeds can be a major
issue in the divorce. I work with them to make it happen quickly and smoothly, so that they can both get on
with their lives.

THE NEWS MEDIA AND "FREE" ADVERTISING

When you read the daily paper or listen to the local
news, do you ever notice that the same "experts" are
constantly quoted in stories? Why do these same people always get the call from the media whenever
there's breaking news? Is it because they know more
than other people in their industry? Probably not.

There are three main reasons why "experts" are con-
tacted often by the press:

1: *They are "good interviews."* They speak candidly
  and directly answer questions. Also, when inter-

viewed for radio or TV, they think and speak in "sound bites." Broadcast media determine if they can air an interview by whether it fits into a thirty-second space. If you can make one or two colorful statements that get right to the point in a few seconds, you will greatly improve your chances of getting quoted on TV or radio.

2:   *They are accessible.* The media do not wait for return calls. When they want to interview you, they want you available within minutes. Expert salespeople go out of their way to make an interview happen as soon as a reporter calls. If the media calls and you are not available almost immediately, you will probably not be called again.

3:   *Most important, they have developed prior relationships with key members of the media.* Like most busy people, reporters are constantly trying to get more done in less time. If they know you are accessible and a good interview, generally an interview with you is easier and safer than contacting an unknown source.

TIME AND *EXTRA*, TOO

By now, my promotional efforts with the news media area really bearing fruit. In November 1995, I was in *Time* magazine. I was on the nationally syndicated television show *Extra*. I've done hundreds of radio interviews on stations across the nation. How did I do it? How did I get interviewed by every local news station in metropolitan Detroit?

Simple. I asked to be there. I hired a public relations firm on a monthly retainer. Their job was to get coverage for me, to get me recognized. In my marketplace, I'm seen as an expert on real estate. If interest rates change, the media call me. If housing sales are slow, they come to me for comment. If housing sales are booming, they interview me.

I'm perceived to be the expert on everything, because I asked to be the expert. I had my PR company send out press releases. I have one to two lunches a month with publishers, editors, and writers. I am networking with these influential people to help build my career.

There are many ways to establish contact with your local media. Invite key reporters or editors to lunch. Give them your marketing kit. Mail or fax the reporter useful information on a regular basis. Follow up with phone calls, but be careful not to become a nuisance.

ALWAYS CREATE REPRINTS

Here's a key rule: Once you are quoted in a story, get reprints. A reprint is actually more valuable than the original article, because you can target who you want to see it. Put it in all your marketing kits. Leave it in your office lobby where visitors can see it. Send it at random to people in your marketplace, with a note saying, "Thought you might be interested in the issue discussed here. . . ."

Unless you have an incredibly generous local newspaper, you'll probably have to create your reprints yourself. If you're short of cash, merely clip out the article, have it photocopied, and send it to everyone in your marketplace. If it's a broadcast interview, get a video or audio tape of the interview, reproduce it, and circulate it as much as you can.

At my office, we go to a lot of trouble over our reprints. We mount the newspaper's masthead at the top of a page, reset the type so that it fits nicely, reproduce either the same photo that ran in the paper or a similar (often better) one. Then we'll get copies made at a local printer. It's cheaper than you may think. I can get 500 to 1,000 black-and-white copies made for $150 to $200, including the typesetting.

For a really special article, you may want to splurge. When *Time* magazine profiled me in its People section, I had 5,000 full-color copies made. I mounted many of those on wall plaques and sent them to friends and clients, with personal notes ("I wouldn't have been in *Time* if it weren't for great customers like you."). I've had more "thank-you" responses to those plaques than to any other promotion I've ever done.

By the way, there was an unexpected bonus. Even though the article about me ran inside the magazine, people come up to me now and say, "I saw your picture on the cover of *Time*." Some even say, "I saw you on the cover of *Money* magazine," even though I've never been in *Money*. The story just grows in the telling. And when people tell me something like that, I just smile and smile.

YOUR BEST LEADS COME FROM YOUR PAST CLIENTS

We've already met my neighbor, auto dealer Mike Riehl. Mike tells me that a top auto salesperson, the kind of person who is selling 250 cars a year, can do almost all of that business strictly from past clients and referrals. Another friend, Joe Vicari, owns seven restaurants in metro Detroit, and Joe tells me that 50 to 60 percent of his clientele are repeat customers. Most successful salespeople, maybe all, can tell similar stories.

So I keep a file of thousands of past clients to whom I mail a newsletter each month. I just keep them up-to-date on my activities. More than 50 percent of my business comes from referrals from past clients. I mail my past clients and ask them for business. I take them out to dinner and give them gifts. They're worth more to me than anything. If I have a past client call me at the same time as a possible new client, I'll work with the past client first.

Recently, I asked another salesperson how often he mailed his past customers. "I never mail them," he told me. Amazing! He was passing up his single greatest source of new sales. I advised him to compose a letter immediately (with his picture on it, of course) and mail every past customer he's ever had.

I've heard it said that it's five times easier to keep an old client than it is to get a new client. Even if something didn't go 100 percent perfect in their transaction, don't put off calling them. They know you were trying to do your best job.

A few years ago, my wife and I started throwing a customer appreciation day each year. First we did it at our home, but it's gotten too big for that. We arrange for hot-air balloon rides and pony rides for kids. It costs me about $10,000 for rides and clowns and pop and hot dogs. I invite all my past clients. I've taken them all to a theme park for a day, but you can have a day at the zoo or the park or rent a baseball stadium for a day.

If you sell airplanes, you should have your party in an airplane hanger; if you sell boats, throw a cruise for your past clients. They're not all going to show up, but I believe this helps maintain your client list and even develop it further. It makes it more rewarding for everyone.

MICKEY MOUSE MARKETING

Whatever you do by way of self-promotion, you've got to outdo what all the other salespeople are doing.

I used to like to pass out my brochure with $2 bills in them, including a little note, "Good job, great service, Ralph Roberts." Now I put Disney Dollars, the play money featuring Mickey Mouse and other characters, with writing on the edges. Whatever you do, you need to look for ways to stand out in the minds of prospective clients.

Years ago, at Sunday open houses, I started to stock the freezer with pint-size cartons of Häagen-Dazs ice cream. I'd tape my business card to each carton. Everybody who stopped at my open house got a pint of ice cream. I figured that they wouldn't want the ice cream to melt, so they'd go right home and put it away instead of going on to another open house. I don't know if it really worked, but it did seem to increase the number of calls to my office on Monday morning.

Another technique I used for a while got me all kinds of free publicity. Since I buy and sell homes for a living, I'm always meeting people who are moving. I bought a big moving van, painted my name on the side, and gave free use of the van to any family for whom I handled their transaction. They'd have to supply the muscle to do the move, but every week my van was out there, a moving billboard for my services. Eventually, the expense of insurance forced me to drop this particular promotion, but it gives you the idea of the kind of thing you need to do.

One woman Realtor I know buys a live Christmas tree for everyone she sells a home to. She delivers it, and it's decorated with little lights and tinsel. She sells about seventy houses a year, so she'll hand out seventy of these trees each year. They don't cost her much, because they're pretty small, maybe a few thousand dollars a year. She's selling homes in the $150,000 to $200,000 range, so she's doing probably $10 million in volume. The investment in trees is small by comparison. Even one commission may cover the entire annual investment in trees. She'll even help each family plant their trees. She tells them that as their family and life together grow, the tree will grow, too. Boy, what a great reminder of that salesperson. The family that gets one will think of her every time they walk out into their yard.

You don't have to copy that idea or one of mine if it's

not right for your market. Be creative. I once met a woman Realtor who stood six feet, two inches tall. I advised her to promote herself as the tallest female agent—get the most for your money, that sort of thing.

DISREGARD WHAT DOESN'T WORK

You've got to try a lot of different things to learn what works. You may have to stick with something for six or nine months before it works. But the rule is this: Disregard it if you find that it doesn't work.

Like refrigerator magnets. Those magnets with your name and face on them. I used them for years, and so do millions of other salespeople. Insurance people do it. Dentists do it. But they don't work. I'm absolutely convinced that refrigerator magnets will never get you a sale.

I've listed houses for sale that had two or three or four refrigerator magnets from other agents attached to the 'fridge holding up pieces of paper. It makes no sense that all these refrigerator magnets are sent out, because no one's ever going to call you because of one.

Whenever I go into someone's home, I look around for that sort of thing. It's always interesting to see how much wasted labor other salespeople go to. They send out calendars and magnets and ink pens. That stuff isn't what gets you sales. Your marketing campaign—the image of you as conveyed in articles or brochures—is what works. Give your customers something of value that they can read and that will make them think of you when they need a salesperson.

If you doubt me, then consider this: Sometimes I'll have my customers sign our sales agreement using a pen left there by a rival salesperson.

IMPROVE YOUR MATERIALS

Just as using some marketing material is better than none at all, using higher quality material is better still. When I was younger, I read every book on personal marketing. I thought I knew everything about the subject. I was fanatical—I would redo all my marketing materials every eighteen months. When I was working for one of the real estate franchises, I had a personal brochure that I was quite fond of. It talked about me and my accomplishments. No one could accuse me of the mistake of not marketing myself.

But I believe now that I was making an error. It wasn't a matter of getting my materials out in the hands of the public. I was doing well with that. It was more a mistake of what I was handing out: standard business cards and a generic brochure that looked like five other salespersons' brochures in my marketplace. It didn't dawn on me at the time, but I was distributing materials identical to what every other salesperson was handing out. If you put our stuff into a big pile, it all looked the same.

HIRING HOBBS/HERDER

So about two years ago, I hired a personal marketing consulting firm—Hobbs/Herder Advertising of Santa

Ana, California—to create a marketing campaign for me. For years, Don Hobbs and Greg Herder had been after me to hire them to create my personal brochure. It seemed like every year we would meet at sales conventions, they would approach me, and I would say, "No thanks." I thought, "I sell more real estate than anyone else, why do I need them?" I thought I knew more than they did about personal marketing.

Well, after I finally lost 100 pounds, I knew it was time to create some new materials. (People kept telling me, "You're not Ralph Roberts, you don't look anything like Ralph Roberts.") I decided to give Hobbs/Herder a chance to create a personal brochure for me.

To make a long story short, I am extremely pleased with my personal brochure. The photos show me not only in business, but at home, too (in one shot, I'm in the middle of my very elaborate toy train set, which is a big hobby of mine). I think my brochure truly captures who I am as a person and as a real estate professional. Many of my friends and superstar salespeople I talk with agree that my personal brochure is "me." That's what I was looking for all along in my personal marketing, but never really found—a way to really stand out from all the generic materials that all agents pass out to consumers.

I've had great success with my new materials, and I took what I learned from the Hobbs/Herder advice and earnestly started using their marketing and lead-generating systems. Now I am selling more real estate, working less time, and having more people call me, because I'm doing personal marketing with high-quality pieces that are tailor-made for me and my marketplace.

If you are going to do a personal brochure (and I hope you will), I urge you not to make the same mistake I did and settle for a cookie-cutter generic brochure that makes you look like just another salesperson.

BROCHURES DO NO GOOD SITTING IN YOUR DESK!

Whether you create your own pieces or hire a consultant to do them for you, don't be afraid to hand them out! You've got to get the word out. If I can share only one secret with you about how I was able to reach a level of selling nearly 600 homes a year, it's this: Pass your brochure out every chance you get. Don't be like some salespeople: They purchase a full-color brochure and other marketing materials and are then afraid to pass them out because they're expensive.

In fact, one or two commissions from sales that result from your marketing materials will pay for your entire effort. Remember, you've got to spend money to make money. You've got to invest in your career to enjoy a giant leap in your production.

TWENTY-FIRST CENTURY PROMOTING

I'm sure that as we move deeper into the twenty-first century, self-promotion is going to become even more important. Selling is getting so competitive and your customer's money so tight that the successful salesperson will be the one who makes a customer feel warm and fuzzy. You've got to make them laugh and look in your eyes and believe in what you're saying.

I have assistants whose job is to send out birthday cards and little greetings to past clients and other people. They just stay in touch with people in a friendly way. I don't like to have my cards lost in the holiday shuffle, so instead of Christmas cards I'll send out after-Christmas cards or Groundhog Day cards. Then I'll run into people at the store and they'll say they got a nice card from my office. I may have no idea what card they're talking about, but I know that it's part of my marketing effort. You've got to set up systems and get people to work for you who will keep those systems going.

NEVER STOP!

Never stop marketing yourself. Every time I go some-where, the car valet gets a good tip and my brochure. It's so important. The other day, I was in a restaurant and I saw a man I thought was the police commissioner from my town. So I started to chat with him. Turns out that he and his wife are retiring to a cottage up north, and within a few minutes, he had bought a ticket to a charity event I'm involved with and talked to me about having me sell his home.

Or here's another one: Right now I'm caught in the middle of a deal that hasn't worked out. A woman homebuyer had given a deposit to a seller, and the sale fell apart. The seller hasn't returned the deposit. I was representing the seller. Well, I saw the buyer, a woman, in a restaurant with her friends having dinner. I know she's not really mad at me. She knows I was trying my best to make the deal work. But I was determined to win her over completely, so I bought dinner for her and her friends. However her dispute comes out, she'll have a positive image of me. And I bet she'll call me again when she needs a salesperson.

Remember, none of this is rocket science. Self-promotion is a tried-and-true activity that all salespeople can do. And it's something that all successful salespeople take very seriously. Good luck.

YOUR CHAPTER 5 CHECKLIST

Let's conclude this chapter with a checklist of what you should be doing to promote yourself. Ask yourself the following questions. If the answer isn't "yes," you've got some more work to do.

✓ Have I got my picture on my business card?

✓ Is my photograph on my letterhead and all correspondence that leaves my office?

✓ Do I reprint all articles about me?

✓ Do I mail reprints to my customers?

✓ Have I worked up a budget for self-promotion activity?

✓ Do I follow this budget?

✓ Do I mail something to my past customers on a regular basis?

✓ Do I routinely send out thank-you cards, birthday wishes, holiday greetings, and similar material to people in my marketplace?

✓ Is my phone number (that is, my direct line) on all the sales material I send or hand out to clients?

✓ Do I call or mail members of the news media on a regular basis?

✓ Have I engaged the services of a professional firm that handles self-promotional activity?

✓ Do I hold a customer-appreciation day at least once a year?

✓ Do I analyze my promotional activities and disregard those that don't work?

✓ Do I constantly seek new ways to promote myself?

6

Camp Out on the Cutting Edge

WHEN IT COMES TO TECHNOLOGY, I'VE NEVER MADE THE classic mistake of resisting it. Quite the opposite, I've always been the first kid on the block to own the latest gadget. I buy the newest clock radio on the market so I can program it to play my CDs and motivational tapes. When I got into my sales career twenty years ago, I was one of the first real estate agents in the country to have a phone in my car. I used to get into an accident once a year leaning over to reach the dialer on the floorboard. No one ever got hurt, but the owner of a body shop became one of my best friends.

If I did make a mistake with technology, it was seeing it only as a toy and not as a weapon or tool to make me more productive and efficient. Today, I understand that technology can help me promote my image in the minds of my clients. In short, it can make me more money. I now understand that I can turn every new technology or product into a tool to better myself as a salesperson or improve the efficiency of operations at my company. Even that old dial system on my first car phone quickly became a tool to help me get more appointments and deals—when it was working.

Technology can be as simple as an extra phone line in your home and as complex as a multistation computer network linked by the latest software. It can include e-mail, the Internet, fax machines, pagers, laptop computers, interactive 800 numbers, and a host of other devices and services. I look around my office today and see a vast array of technological breakthroughs. Fax machines—before these marvels we used to courier everything back and forth, back and forth. I have a pager. I have two phones on my desk and a cellular phone in my briefcase. I have a calculator and a digital measuring device to measure rooms in homes. I have a laptop computer. There are two microcassette recorders in my briefcase for documenting ideas. I have my own Web page at www.ralphroberts.com. When it comes to technology, I've tried just about everything. I'll be discussing the various tools and what they can do for you in this chapter.

WHY SO MANY RESIST

Unfortunately, too many salespeople resist technology, mostly out of fear. That's so tragic. To fear technology only denies you an opportunity to better yourself.

Many people say that they're too dumb to learn a new technology, but they're wrong. We use technology all the time without ever thinking about it. The automobile you drive is probably as complex as a new computer (in fact, most cars today depend on computer chips to operate). Your telephone is a technological device. Even your ballpoint pen was a technological breakthrough at one time. The difference, of course, is that these are older technologies that we all grew up using. But there's nothing inherently more difficult about a newer technology; all it takes is practice to get used to it.

Another objection people have to technology is that it's expensive. But my friend Pat Zaby, a veteran salesperson who designs software for the sales profession, has the answer to that one. "You have probably heard the expression, 'If you think education is expensive, you ought to try ignorance.'" The same can be applied to technology. As Pat says, if you think computers and software are expensive, you ought to consider the sales you lost because you weren't utilizing the technology.

A third objection to new technology is that it doesn't work like it should. And, yes, this can be the case, especially when technology is new. When pagers came out, I rushed out and got one of those pagers where you can hear the people speaking through it. How I hated that thing! I'd be sitting in a restaurant and hear someone talking through my belt, or if I had it in my coat pocket, I could hear someone talking, and I couldn't shut the darn thing off. I also remember that our first computers gave us our multiple listing service printouts on this really terrible paper. I don't know what it was called, but if you set it down on your desk for two hours, pretty soon the ink faded away and the information wasn't there. Sometimes technology works, and sometimes it doesn't. The bottom line is you want to be sure it is working *for* you and not against you.

HOW IT CAN WORK FOR YOU

To illustrate how much technology can do for you, let me tell you about one of my neighbors in metropolitan Detroit. Peg Ostby founded her travel business, Creative Cruises, in 1988. Within six years, she had built it to $500,000 a year in sales. Then she found the right sales-automation computer program. She *doubled* her business in less than eighteen months. Peg has only four full-time employees at Creative Cruises, including herself. But these four people manage a client database of nearly 10,000 names.

For example, Peg does a lot of business with beauty salons. With her computer program, she can write a "thank-you" letter to 500 salon operators who took one of her cruises. She'll touch a button and fifteen minutes later she'll have 500 letters ready to mail with the names merged. Touch another button, and she's got 500 envelopes. Touch another, and the "history" function of her program enters a notice that the letter was sent on each client's file. A calendar function can let Peg know when it's time to follow up the letters with a phone call. And she can customize her program to fit her particular needs very easily. Peg paid about

$1,000 for a four-user license, meaning the program runs on four PCs in her office. The gains she's made have long since paid back her investment many times over.

Salespeople who don't use the latest technology are looking for trouble. In real estate, we're probably going to lose more than half the salespeople now in business by early in the next century. That's less than five years away. Pretty soon now, people are going to be buying houses without looking at them. They'll be viewing homes on a computer screen. While they're looking at a computer screen, they'll be applying for their loan. Through the fax machine will come their loan documents, and they'll sign them and leave owning a house.

It's scary for a lot of salespeople, but the ones who embrace the new technology will prosper. As Pat Zaby says, "Technology can make the difference between a moderate income in sales and a great income."

So let's get started. Even if you've never used a computer or sent an e-mail message, if you start today, you'll still be ahead of the field. Not all salespeople use computers and other new technologies to boost their sales. Only the successful do.

VOICE MAIL AND OTHER PHONE SERVICES

When it comes to technology, there's low-level investments and high-level investments. Let's start with some low-level stuff. Take voice mail and answering machines. First, if you're not using one of these now, you must start immediately. The number of calls—the amount of sales—that you'll miss by not using this technology can put you out of business.

Many people who use voice mail don't use it correctly. Many salespeople put a greeting on their voice mail and leave it there for five years. Some people let their kids do the greeting at home. The kids have grown and gone off to college, and the parents still haven't changed their greeting.

To be a superstar, you need to see voice mail as another proactive tool that will help you succeed. Many top salespeople change their greetings every morning. This lets callers know that you're in the office and interested in their calls. Other features are available that let you couple it with a pager, so that a caller can leave you a message which will then page you to let you know it's there. You can also link your pager and voice mail to features like call forwarding.

Phone features are available that let us do all sorts of things. Pizza stores can now invest in a directory technology, similar to caller ID, that instantly lists the name, address, and previous order history of each caller on a computer screen. So a clerk can greet each call with something like: "Well, good evening, Mr. Jones, last time you ordered the double pepperoni with anchovies. Would you like that same order again?" That's quite a surprise for their customers, and it really establishes goodwill. Or suppose you run a computer company and a regular customer calls in to buy a modem. Your clerk can pull up the customer's purchase history and say, "Ms. Smith, I see you're still using version 2.0 of that software. The upgrade is in. Would you like us to include that with your order?" This sort of technology turns everyone who answers your phone into a salesperson.

Take advantage of all these features, or at least explore them. One secret of successful use of technology is that there are almost always more features to a given technology than we're ever aware of.

Nowhere is that more true than with computers.

COMPUTERS

A few years ago, the *Harvard Business Review* published a study on computers and selling. It said that you can make your business at least 30 percent more efficient by using the right sales-automation software. I think it may be even higher. How much more money would you make if you were 30 percent more efficient? Or how much more time off would you have for your family, friends, and hobbies?

I use computers and software to supercharge my marketing efforts and lead-generating systems. I have one program that tracks what we call "expireds," which are listings of homes that automatically come off the market at a certain date. I just turn on my computer, execute the program, and it searches through the multiple listing service for listings about to expire. The same system tracks "for sale by owner" homes on the market. I mean, you still have to make the phone calls, stuff the envelopes, and do the follow up, but what a powerful tool to use in these lead-generating systems. It's incredible. When my staff comes into work, they turn on their computers and there's work already there for them to do.

There are basically three, or possibly four, types of computer software that salespeople need to use. They are, first, a *contact management* program to keep track of people, dates, appointments, and events; second, a *presentation* program to create persuasive materials to convince buyers and sellers to do business with you; third, a *financial analysis* program to provide data for buyers and sellers trying to make their decisions; and fourth, possibly a program such as Quicken to help you track your personal finances.

Let's talk about the first three types.

CONTACT MANAGEMENT PROGRAMS

A contact management program is one that keeps track of people and events. It's primary purpose is prospecting for leads. These software programs usually include a database, a word processor, and a calendar. These different functions are linked so that the information flows seamlessly from one task to another. A good program will provide room for not only the basic names, addresses, and phone numbers of your clients, but also space to keep track of important information about each.

One valuable feature of contact managers is their ability to sort the names, not only alphabetically or by address, zip code, or phone number, but by a number of ways that the salesperson defines. You might, for example, sort your database into lists of past clients, relatives and friends, new prospects, etc.

Another important feature alerts you that it's time to contact your clients again. You the salesperson will program in what the schedule should be, and then the program will remind you like an alarm clock when a contact is due. The best programs will take a prewritten letter or postcard, merge it with your address list, and send it to the printer. All you have to do is say okay when the computer asks if you want to go ahead.

Some other features: Contact managers can store hundreds of sample client letters and they can print your mailing labels, saving you hundreds of hours of time.

There are many good programs on the market. Peg Ostby uses a contact manager program called GoldMine for Windows. At my own firm, we use ACT! software by Symantec Corp. We manage a database of thousands of clients and potential clients. I do mass mailing to more than 50,000 households in my market several times a year. Without ACT!, we'd never be nearly as efficient as we are.

ACT! and GoldMine are priced about the same— roughly $275 for an individual user and up to $1,000 for a four- or five-user license. ACT! is available in both Windows and Macintosh versions.

Richard Bohn, a Seattle-based expert whose newsletter, *Sales Automation Success*, tracks these trends, has a list of about sixty-five different programs, each catering to a different set of needs. Some will manage your list of clients, while others will help you draw up proposals. Bohn has published a book, *Sales Automation Software Compendium*, which you may want to look at. (It's 332 pages and costs $97. It's available from Bohn's company, The Denali Group, 2815 N.W. Pine Cone Drive, Issaquah, Washington, 98027-8698, phone: 206-392-3514.)

PRESENTATION PROGRAMS

If a contact management program provides the guts of what you need, a presentation program lets you make it all look super. Pat Zaby, who has designed the Prep Presentations program for the real estate business, puts it this way: A contact manager is like the engine and drive train of a car, while a presentation program is the body and interior. The mechanical system gets you there, but what really impresses people are the styling and condition.

In short, a presentation program is like a desktop publisher that has all the design work already done. With a little personalizing of the standard products, a salesperson can have high-quality, persuasive presentations in minutes. Sometimes it's as simple as a checklist, other times a colorful brochure. Naturally, different sales professions need different programs, as you can hardly expect a program written for Realtors to help a car salesperson. But more and more of these programs are entering the market each year. You can easily learn what's the latest in your particular field by calling your national trade group.

Once you get your presentations prepared, you can

print them out on paper or create your own slide show on your laptop computer. Imagine that you're in your client's home and, instead of pulling out tattered photographs of your product, you flip open your laptop computer, touch a few keystrokes, and dazzling full-color text and photos blossom into view. It's a real winner.

FINANCIAL ANALYSIS PROGRAMS

A confused client seldom buys. To sell more products, you need to lessen your customer's misgivings, not add to them. A financial analysis program enables you to provide your client with the data needed to make a decision.

For example, in real estate, we now have programs that will prequalify a buyer for a mortgage, broken down by their income level and what type of loan they're seeking, such as FHA, VA, conventional loans, or whatever. These programs can estimate closing costs and show a homeowner what will happen if they increase their monthly payments against the principal. They can compare adjustable-rate versus fixed-rate loans. These and other factors will go a long way toward helping buyers decide what they can afford to do. Without such knowledge, they most likely won't be buying at all.

It's an old axiom that knowledge equals power. Think how powerful you'll be when you can dazzle your clients with data instead of trying to baffle them with BS.

INTERACTIVE 800 NUMBERS

Everyone has probably dialed an 800 number, and quite a few sales offices now offer them to clients as a convenience. However, only a handful use the interactive variety. In fact, I've just begun to use one in my own office, but I'm already impressed by the power of this technology to boost my revenues.

Basically, an interactive 800 number is one that offers callers a menu of choices, such as ordering a report on market conditions or a consumer's guide on how to shop for a car or a computer. The consumer can order any of these items by pressing a key on their phone, then entering their fax number or leaving their name and address on voice mail.

But here's the really exciting feature: This technology also "captures" the caller's name and phone number through a system similar to caller ID. So even if all the caller does is browse through the menu and hang up, we still know who they are. We can call them back later, or, since we have their name and phone number, we can get their address and mail them our brochures. If they were interested enough to call our office, even out of curiosity, calling them back is more productive than simply cold calling. They've already prequalified themselves as a prospect just by calling our number in the first place.

If the callers enter their own fax number, they'll receive an instant fax-back feature sheet with any information that we want to send them—such as maps, personal promotions, mortgage financing guidelines, whatever I want them to see immediately.

Another feature: If a caller presses a key to ask for mortgage information, the system automatically pages my assistant in charge of our mortgage business. He'll call them back within minutes. It's an awesome response time—a live call-back within moments of a customer's call to our 800 number.

Another good feature: It lets me know which of my advertisements are working. The caller touches in a code that he or she read in the ad. This lets me identify which ads are getting a response. My advertising is more accountable this way.

The system we use at my office is called 800 Powerline. It's designed by a company called ARCH Telecom, based in Houston, Texas. Steve Cortez, their director of sales, tells me the system works well for all sorts of independent salespeople. Some of their best customers are insurance agents, auto dealerships, and small computer shops—any salesperson who needs an edge on their larger competition. One of the things I like about it is that it leaves me with complete control. For example, by pressing zero a caller can be transferred to my home, office, car, or portable phone. But *I* decide where these zero-transfer calls will be sent. *I'm* always in control on my system. (If you want to talk to ARCH Telecom about the 800 Powerline system, Steve's direct number is 1-800-882-9155.)

Some salespeople don't like this technology. They complain that it doesn't capture calls from cellular phones, or that if someone calls your office from a pay phone or a corporation, it's a waste of time trying to call back. Maybe so, but think of it this way. Suppose just 10 percent of your callers turn into solid leads. That's more than enough to pay back the cost of your investment.

E-MAIL

Recently, I attended a real estate convention in Florida and during one session on technology, the moderator asked how many people had ever sent an e-mail message. Only about half the people in the room raised their hands. That's probably typical of most Americans, but these were among the leading real estate salespeople in the nation.

By contrast, e-mail is another one of my favorites. E-mail is like a sticky note that doesn't get lost, doesn't fall off the wall, and doesn't get stuck under stacks of papers. What an effective way it is to communicate with staff and clients.

But e-mail can be much more than just an electronic note. Programs now exist that permit salespeople to spice up their e-mail with multimedia graphics and sound. One such program is called Eudora Pro that markets for about $80. It includes sample greeting cards to say thank you and other messages. When your client receives your e-mail, they click on the appropriate spot and, provided they have a computer equipped for multimedia displays, up pops a greeting card that opens before their eyes to the accompaniment of a jingle. You can even personalize your card with your own photo or the photo of your product. Not everyone has a multimedia computer, but so many people are upgrading to them that you're already behind the curve if you don't explore this technology.

E-mail is useful in other ways. In my office, we're also using e-mail to save money we'd normally spend creating our monthly *Homes* magazines. Until recently, when we printed up our magazines, we'd have to ship the color photos of homes for sale to a printer. Now, we can send our color photos to an out-of-state printer via e-mail. It's cheaper and faster and, because distance is no longer a barrier, we can shop for a better rate on the printing of our magazine.

We can also create lists of clients and then mass-mail messages to everyone at once. Suppose you have a thousand clients in your e-mail address book. What a terrific, cost-effective way to reach so many people! Just a few keystrokes and you can do a mass mailing that might cost you hundreds of dollars and many hours of time if you used surface mail.

E-mail illustrates one of the keys about technology: There are always more ways to use it than we think. Remember, when it comes to computer technology, a year ago is ancient history. Stay current with what's happening out there. It will pay dividends.

WEB SITES

The Internet and the World Wide Web are all the rage now, and many a salesperson in my field has his or her own Web page. Unfortunately, some 90 percent of these Web pages are worthless! They may gratify the ego of the salesperson who created them, but they do little or nothing to generate leads or income.

A good Web site must be interactive. A client who visits your site must be able to do more than browse through a list of your current products. Visitors must be able to ask for and receive information and discover a vast array of data that will help them make their buying decisions.

For example, one of the keys to any good real estate purchases is the quality of the local schools. Any real estate salesperson ought to include information about the local schools in a Web site. You may, for example, offer a hypertext link to the local school board's own Web page. Be careful, however: You want to keep people in your page, not send them off somewhere else. It's better to design a page that includes all the relevant data instead of just giving visitors a map to go somewhere else.

A good Web page ought to run you no more than $1,000. Even for $500, you can get a pretty good basic package. There are all kinds of people and companies out there designing Web pages. Shop around a bit and find one whose products and price suit your needs.

Many salespeople make the mistake of placing their Web page under the umbrella of a larger organization, such as a national sales group or a local chamber of commerce. You'll get lost that way. You ought to set up your own separate and distinct Web site. Your designer will know how to do this. And then how do you get people to know how to reach your site? By advertising. Put your Web site address (and your e-mail address, too) on every piece of paper that leaves your office, just as you list your name and phone number.

Once you create your page, you'll also need to get your site linked with the various search engines that consumers use to cruise the Web. So if someone punches in the keywords "Detroit" and "real estate," my site will be among the ones to pop up.

Just recently, I found another service I like. It's called Realty Connection. Based in Dallas, Texas, this firm provides the technology to let me set up a unique Web site for each and every customer. Say a buyer is interested in three-bedroom ranch homes in Warren, Michigan. I can load all the available information about such homes on to a Web page accessed only by this specific client, who uses a password I give them. I'll include data on moving companies, schools, shopping, transportation, and amenities such as parks and playgrounds. The buyers can shop for a home by browsing this customized Web page in the privacy of their home.

These sorts of services are becoming available in many parts of the sales world. If you'd like to learn more about this one, you can call Realty Connection's president, Jody Lane, at 888-888-3485 or check them out at realtyconnection.com on the Web.

CAMP OUT ON THE CUTTING EDGE

Even as I write this book, new technologies are changing the way salespeople do business. We now have wristwatches on the market that will let you hold up the watch in front of your computer screen to automatically capture your appointment schedule off your computer, so that your watch beeps you at certain times of the day. In my office, we're already using the new digital cameras; instead of printing paper copies of photos of homes we have for sale, we simply plug our camera into a video monitor and show our photos that way. It's very impressive, and I'm sure this will become yet another tool used by successful salespeople in years to come.

The best sales operations use all of these technologies in combination. My friend Jerry Van Goethem (I mentioned his brother Bob earlier) runs the Uniglobe Eastside Travel franchise here in Detroit. His staff uses technology in many forms. They utilize computerized databases to keep track of which clients prefer aisle seats or window seats and which require special diets. Their technology will not only book airline travel, but also reserve rental cars and hotel rooms. And Jerry combines this state-of-the-art technology with some old-fashioned services, like same-day delivery of tickets to your office.

If you make it a habit to look at every new technological breakthrough as a potential time-saver, money-maker, or marketing tool, then you are in the right mind-set for success in the twenty-first century. That old car phone, the talking pager, and the MLS paper with the disappearing ink all improved with time. Now each is an important marketing and servicing tool. I love technology. Don't you?

YOUR CHAPTER 6 CHECKLIST

✓ Do I put off buying technology because of the expense or difficulty of learning it?

✓ Have I analyzed how new technology may benefit me and my business?

✓ Do I change my voice mail greeting daily or at least often enough to keep it fresh?

✓ Do I use a computer in my business? Have I explored the different kinds of sales automation software, i.e., contact management, presentation, and financial analysis programs?

✓ Have I looked into whether an interactive 800 number would help my business? If I already have one, am I getting the most out of it?

✓ Do I have a strategy for using e-mail? Or do I just use it occasionally to send or answer personal notes?

✓ Do I have my own Web site? Have I explored how I can go about creating one?

✓ Do I have a financial budget for investment in new technology? If not, it's time to create one.

7

Systems Can Set You Free

A COUPLE OF YEARS AGO, A FRIEND, ALLAN DOMB OF Philadelphia, urged me to open my own mortgage company. Allan is the top condominium salesman in the world. He works exclusively in a marketplace of about a dozen high-rise condo buildings, a market of some 5,500 units with a 10 percent annual turnover. Allan controls more than an 80 percent share of this market, and his income runs well into the six figures. So I listened when he told me, "Ralph, if you don't open a mortgage company, I'll come over there and open it up for you!"

Allan had learned that providing mortgages for homebuyers is a natural outgrowth of a Realtor's job. We're always referring our customers to banks and other mortgage lenders. Why not provide the mortgages ourselves and capture that revenue stream? It was an excellent—and very lucrative—suggestion, and I quickly acted on it.

But I found that you can't just open a mortgage company on the back of an envelope. You need to plan for it, hire the right people, train them to run it, and oversee it in operation. You need those assistants and technology that I talked about earlier. In other words, you need to set up a system.

TRACKING TRANSACTIONS

For a guy who's naturally as disorganized as me—my wife claims that I probably have attention deficit disorder, so I've thought of putting ADD on my business card as a credential, you know, Ralph Roberts, GRS, GRI, ADD—I've created really great systems. My company now runs on these systems. Probably half the volume we do comes from having the right systems in place.

Of all the reasons salespeople come to Detroit to shadow me, I'd say the main one is they want to understand my systems. How, they wonder, do I track more than 500 transactions a year?

The answer is simple: Systems. Let's take an example. A homeowner calls my office because they need to sell their house. Instead of just taking their number, my assistants immediately do two things: They send out our company brochure and schedule an appointment. The appointment goes into my planner and an assistant gets all the forms ready for me. An assistant will confirm the appointment a few hours in advance so I don't go on any dry calls. When I get back to the office with the listing—and I almost always get the listing—another assistant takes the forms and starts the ball rolling on everything else, posting the listing on our computer, advertising it, photographing the home. *All these steps happen automatically.* We've created the systems and hired and trained the staff to make them happen.

Systems don't remain static. We are constantly tweaking and improving them so they make things easier for our staff and more effective for our customers.

BLUE FOLDERS, RED FOLDERS

A system can be as simple as using blue file folders for buyers and red file folders for sellers. A system is nothing more than a way to help you keep track of your business. Your systems can include checklists, form letters, schedules, and worksheets. As your business grows in complexity, so will your systems.

Take Joe Hafner, who manages my public relations effort. Joe handles the calls that come in when people want to buy one of the professional products we offer to other salespeople, such as our cassette tapes. Joe keeps a checklist taped to the wall by his phone. It reminds him of all the questions he needs to ask to complete each order, including the expiration date of the caller's credit card. That checklist is a system, a way of helping Joe get his job done.

All the systems in my office range from simple ones

like that to fairly complex ones. The important thing for *you* to do is to start creating your own. No matter what you sell, cosmetics to computers, there are constants. You need to prospect for clients. You need to handle the paperwork. You need to cultivate past clients. For all of these, you can set up systems—organized processes for handling each chore.

ALL THE LITTLE STEPS

In my industry, as no doubt in yours, there are many little steps that must take place in a transaction. When a house is sold, credit needs to be checked, homes need to be inspected, a closing date needs to be scheduled. If I had to do my main job—working with buyers and sellers—*and* do all that other stuff, I couldn't possibly handle the volume I do. So I hire top-notch assistants to help me, and I create the systems—the paperwork flow—so that everything runs like clockwork.

To give you a simple blueprint for creating systems, it goes like this:

1. Do a step-by-step analysis of each process in your business, from prospecting to closing the deal.

2. Reduce each part of this process to a checklist. Your checklists should include every step that's needed to complete each stage.

3. Hire and train assistants who will follow the checklist for each and every transaction.

KEEPING ME OUT OF IT

Let me give you an example. Lisa is the staff person in my office who coordinates all our closings. She'll do as many as seventy closings in a single month—not bad for someone who's just twenty-one years old. Anyway, Lisa has a variety of checklists that go into every single file. There can be dozens of items, from getting the home inspected to making sure both buyer and seller show up at closing time. Since we deal with so many transactions, Lisa has a few dozen open files on her desk at any given time, that is, deals that are between initial agreement and final closing. And she'll go over those files in detail every week to make sure nothing slips through the cracks.

Do I need to be involved in all those details? Hardly. Lisa does her best to keep me out of the process entirely. She says it runs better that way!

It's important to let your assistants stamp their own personality onto your systems. Lisa, for example, noticed that she was constantly looking in some files just to see if they were open or closed. With hundreds of files each year, she can't keep track of them all in her head. So to save the trouble of pulling each file and leafing through it, she created a little sticker. It's a square that goes on the top right corner of each file that's closed. It notes when the file was completed. Lisa can tell just by glancing at the folder whether it's open or closed, and she doesn't have to even pull the file from the file cabinet. Lisa came up with this idea on her own, and it makes her life easier.

NOTHING THROUGH THE CRACKS

Visitors to our office are often surprised at how many systems I use. We have about two dozen going in our office at any time, covering all aspects of our business. In real estate, that means I have one system for buyers, another for sellers; one for FSBOs, another for property we're buying for investment. There is a system to manage a condominium project that I own, and another to run my public relations operations. And, of course, I have one to write this book.

We try to let nothing fall through the cracks. Every day, I dictate memos to my secretary, Betty, about matters big and small, and I leave the little cassette tape with these memos in her in-basket each morning. She'll transcribe them, forward a copy to the appropriate staffer, and file a copy in the ring binder we use to keep track of each system. I've also set up weekly meetings with all my department heads. At those meetings, we go over our projects for the week and our past performance.

NOT PERFECT, BUT GOOD

I won't kid you and say all my systems are perfect. They're not. We make mistakes, too. We're always tinkering with our systems. We create new ones all the time. They can be real hard to set up, but eventually they run well. The proof is in the volume that I do. No one could possibly handle more than 500 home sales a year without excellent systems.

So take your time, set up your systems, and they'll work like magic. If you do things methodically, you can get to the next level.

PLAN THE WORK, WORK THE PLAN

Of course, it's hard to know what systems to create until you know where you want to go. In a general sense, sure, you know you want to sell more product and make more money. But if you analyze your goals, both financial and personal, you'll come up with a much clearer idea of how to manage your business.

I'm a little ashamed to admit it, but I didn't write my first business plan until less than five years ago. It was on a pad of yellow legal paper. It was less than ten sheets in length, handwritten.

At the time, I was running a business in excess of $50 million a year, and I'm writing on yellow sheets? I went to the bank to get a credit line to buy some foreclosed homes. The banker said, "Let me see a copy of your business plan." I gave it to him. He said, "Well, it's good, but is this how you keep your business plan?" I said, "Well, that's the written copy, I could show you the typed copy, but we keep it back at the office for the staff."

I didn't have a typed copy. I didn't have it, and the staff didn't know what I was going to do or where we were going. Just repeating this scenario makes me shudder.

BEGINNING TO CHANGE

A few years ago, superstar salesman Stanley Mills from Memphis, Tennessee, visited me and my family during the week between Christmas and New Year's. We spent a week writing a business plan. That one week spent developing that business plan changed my life forever.

Well, you know me. When I see something good, I try to multiply it and keep it going. This past year, I started my business plan at Thanksgiving and finished it just after the first of the year. My business plan is now 109 pages, and it has everything, including details of how much I'm going to generate an hour. Now my staff, my secretary, the receptionist, everybody at the company knows that when Ralph is working, he's got to be doing the most dollar-productive thing. They realize that when I'm working, it pays everybody. So if they get the water bill and it needs to get paid, or something gets dropped off, I don't get bothered with it. They know they need to handle it. They know where we're going and how we're going to get there.

My staff has learned to protect me from myself. Not long ago, we were cleaning out our office building, and I wanted to make it a team-building exercise with everyone involved. Well, there were a couple of fence posts lying in the basement, the ones with the concrete around the bases, and some of our guys were busting up the concrete so we could get rid of the poles. It looked like fun, so I went over there and took a sledge and started hammering. Jane, who's been with me eleven years, came up to me and said, "Ralph, you're our rainmaker, if you get hurt none of us work, so why don't you let the guys do that."

YOU'RE A BUSINESS, NOT AN EMPLOYEE

To this day, I find it incredible that I worked so many years without a business plan. You see, now it seems crystal-clear to me how important a business plan and goals are to a successful salesperson. Years ago, I didn't see it. But you know what? Without a plan and goals, you run the risk of being like a motorboat without a rudder. You end up going in circles or in random and ineffective directions.

So whether you are a salesperson, sales manager, or an owner of your own company, you are an entrepreneur and you need to have a business plan. You need to put down what you're going to do. One of the important benefits of writing a business plan should be getting a grasp on what you should be making an hour. An understanding of what your time is actually worth is essential. Once you begin to truly understand that, you'll hopefully see how ridiculous it is for you to do clerical work that you can delegate.

Allan Domb, the condo salesman, makes 100 phone calls a day. He's got two secretaries helping him dial the numbers so he doesn't lose any time. And as he's making his 100 calls a day, Allan rates each call as to what it's worth to him. This call is a $1,000 call, this one a $500 call, and this one a $50 call. So he does the $1,000 call first, then works down the list. He does the most dollar-productive activity first, and so should you. The next time you're making copies, paying the gas bill, or stuffing envelopes, you'll start realizing you should be paying someone a few dollars an hour to take care of this simple, no-brainer, time-consuming stuff instead of devoting your incredibly valuable time to it. At least try to get into this frame of mind.

START SMALL, BUT START

In the first year, a person who opens a sandwich shop may have to sweep the floors, wipe the tables, and make the sandwiches, in addition to doing the important things like taking inventory and ordering supplies, paying the rent and taxes, and figuring out the menu. But his or her goal or business plan should cover how to generate enough business to hire people to do this work so he or she can concentrate on building the business and expanding to a second shop—or starting a franchise. Food for thought: Does the person running the little sandwich shop in the strip mall have a better business plan than salespeople who are, by the claims on their advertisements, multimillion-dollar producers?

I like to go out and speak to people across the nation at least once a month. From my business plan, I know how much business I stand to lose if I'm away speaking. That's one of the ways I set my speaking fees—by how many houses I would have sold, how much business is going to transpire while I'm away. I do have systems in place that allow me to sell houses while I'm away. I have capable employees handling all aspects of my business. It's all part of my business plan.

GOALS AND STRATEGIES

Hopefully, you are getting the picture of how important I think systems and a business plan are to your financial success. They don't have to be complicated. You basically need to outline your goals, workload, and what your strategies are to attain your ends. You don't need to have incredibly complex strategies, and you don't need to set outrageous and unattainable goals.

Remember my buyer's assistant who lost it when I said we were going to try to hit 200 homes from 152? Well, perhaps he would still be working for me if he had read my business plan and seen the simple and logical step-by-step plan that shows how to achieve that goal by breaking it down into small steps.

My goals aren't, "Sell over ten houses a week." That's not how I break it down. I break it down as small as I possibly can. For example, I want to break it down into four FSBOs a month, six expired listings a month, and eight foreclosures a month. I divide it into departments.

Suppose your goal is to sell 240 cars this year. If you look at it that way, it sounds like a monumental task. So break it down to just 20 per month. That sounds a little easier, but it's still somewhat daunting. So let's break it down further to one car per day if you work a five-day week. One car per day doesn't seem too difficult, but take it a step further. How many prospects do you have to approach to sell one car? For the sake of this example, let's say that, on average, you need to have eighteen quality presentations to prospects to sell one car. That means you have to meet with just two prospects each hour of each day you work. How's that for getting you focused? If you just meet with two prospects every hour that you work, you can put yourself on pace to sell 240 cars this year.

Making your goals as simple as possible makes them more attainable. It also helps you realize whether or not they are realistic goals. Maybe your current systems only allow you to meet with one customer per hour; maybe you're on pace to sell only 120 cars this year. But what if you could hire a part-time assistant for $1,000 a month to handle administrative tasks and paperwork? Would that allow you to meet with two—or even three—customers per hour? Would it be worth $12,000 a year to double or even triple your business? Do you see the power of planning, goal setting, and simplifying? It's the only way to get a clear picture of where you are and, more important, how to get to where you want to be.

Your systems and business plan should cover everything. Your plan should even include your personal goals, like taking off to visit your daughter's school. What do you need to do to make it happen?

I made the mistake of not writing business plans early on in my career. Hopefully, you will sit down tonight and begin writing your first plan. You'll be amazed at what it will do for your career and earnings.

YOUR CHAPTER 7 CHECKLIST

✓ Have I performed a step-by-step analysis of each process in my business?

✓ Have I reduced each part of this process to a checklist, complete with the detailed steps that make up each stage?

✓ Have I trained my assistants to follow the checklist for each and every transaction?

✓ Do I allow my assistants to customize my systems to fit their own work habits?

✓ Have I developed systems to cover my prospecting, paperwork flow, promotional activities, and all other aspects of my business?

✓ Do I have a business plan?

✓ Is my business plan written down? Is it available for my employees and advisers to read and understand?

✓ Does my business plan outline my goals, both short-term and long-term?

✓ Does it go into detail about my sources of income, expenses, and schedule?

✓ Do I follow my plan or amend it if I find I can't follow it?

8

People Skills and the Sales Call

LET ME TELL YOU A STORY ABOUT ONE OF MY FAVORITE SALES calls. In this one, though, I wasn't the salesperson, but the customer.

Living and working in Motown, the auto capital of the world, virtually all of my customers work for some part of the auto industry. Naturally, I always drive an American-made vehicle. But one time, several years ago, I decided I wanted to buy a Jaguar. It's one of the most beautiful cars on the road. I thought it would be a great reward for all my hard work. I knew I would have to save for it, since I only pay cash for cars, so I went to the dealership to see the cars and get enthused about this new goal.

Well, there I met one of the world's great salesmen. He charmed me with his knowledge and passion for this car. He obviously loved Jaguars himself, and it was a pleasure just to watch him work. After our test drive, he concluded his sales presentation by running his hand across the leather dashboard and saying, in a very dramatic voice, "You see that leather? *None of the cows that gave that leather ever snagged on barbed wire.*" And as I ran my hand across the leather, I had to admit that there was nary a snag or blemish. This salesman made learning about the cars so much fun that I wanted one right then and there.

Well, I took his brochures, clipped out the photographs of the car, and put them over my desk to remind me of my goal. A few months later, when I had earned the cash to pay for the car, I went back to that dealership, check in hand. But the salesman was gone. He had left for another dealership. What a disappointment! I realized then I didn't just want to buy the car. I wanted to buy it from *him*. I never did buy a Jaguar, not to this day.

THAT ALL-IMPORTANT MAGIC

That's how powerful the magic is between a salesperson and a customer. That's the magic you need to make happen. You can't reduce that magic to a canned formula. When I was younger and starting out, I had a whole series of prescripted remarks, gags, and lead-ins that I'd learned in seminars. My very first listing presentations were horror stories—an overenthusiastic eighteen year old in a bad suit parroting a series of prescripted lines. But over the years, I've learned that every customer and every situation is unique. I soon understood that I had to establish a natural rapport with my customers in order to succeed. My job is to learn each customer's individual needs, then adapt my style to them.

Up to this point of this book, I've talked about how you need to use boosters like assistants, technology, systems, and personal marketing. I don't want to give the impression that the sales call is an afterthought. On the contrary, all the other things we've gone over so far merely free you up to work with your customers. The sales call is where it all comes together. This is your ground-zero moment.

We need to sell the customer not just on the product—most products, after all, sell themselves—but on the importance of using our services. There are lots of salespeople out there making a pitch to your customer. Why should someone choose you?

In this chapter, I'll tell you how I approach my sales calls. The important thing to understand is how all the tiny details can add up to a winning effort.

Step One: Service Comes First, Not Last

There's a wonderful story told about a Nordstrom's department store that once opened in Alaska. Shortly after the store opened, an irate customer brought back some defective snow tires. The salesperson didn't hesitate, but immediately took back the tires and refunded the money. The point of the story? *Nordstrom's doesn't sell snow tires.* What happened was that Nordstrom's had moved into an existing building that had once housed a tire store. The customer had bought the snow tires there from the previous business, but service is so much a part of the Nordstrom's philosophy that the store was willing to take back a product they hadn't even sold.

Chris Younker manages the Nordstrom store in metropolitan Detroit. She tells me that Nordstrom's lives and breathes the service philosophy, even if it means losing a sale now and then.

"We want these customers back," she told me. "If we intimidate them and sell them stuff they don't need, they won't be back."

I couldn't agree more. You can look at unethical behavior as ripples on a pond—they'll just keep expanding out into your future. You'll never escape the consequences. As a salesperson, you've got to take your own financial gain out of a transaction and think only what's best for your customer. The customer loyalty you create will repay you again and again.

With that attitude firmly in place, we can now look at some of the specifics of the sales call.

Step Two: The Silent Salesman

All my sales calls begin before I get to the door. As soon as the customer calls my office to ask for an appointment, my receptionist makes sure that one of my complete media kits gets delivered to their home. This kit is our "silent salesman." It contains my picture, my press clippings, and information about my company and my assistants.

Years ago, I used to do two-hour sales calls, and most of that time was eaten up telling the customer about my company. Now our kit answers all those questions in advance. It frees me to get right to the job of finding out what's on the customer's mind. Another advantage of my approach is that other salespeople rarely go to this much trouble. That puts me one up on them.

No matter what industry you're in, you'll always have some product literature or company background you can hand out. And make sure your business card or personal brochure is with the package.

I always have my secretary confirm all my appointments in advance. If it's a morning sales call, she'll confirm the night before. If it's an afternoon sales call, she'll confirm that morning. You don't want to go on a dry call, so confirm, confirm, confirm.

TIMING CAN BE YOUR BEST FRIEND

If possible, I try to be either the first or last salesperson my customer talks to. Those are the positions at which the customer is most ready to make a decision.

In my business, many people who are getting ready to sell a home may interview five or six salespeople before settling on one to represent them. I've found that there's a 70 percent chance I'll get the listing if I'm the first salesperson they talk to. I have a 95 percent chance if I'm last in. But in between, my odds slip to between 40 and 50 percent.

How come? Well, if I'm the first, I know I can make

such a good presentation that the customer will list with me and cancel all the other appointments. If I'm last, I can make the customer forget all the others who came before. But in the middle, the customer is usually determined to interview everybody. So my staff has learned to position me first or last when making appointments.

When I do find myself stuck in the middle, there's a technique that I use to overcome the odds. I'll find out when the next salesperson's appointment will take place. Then I'll have some flowers or a plant or a pie delivered to the client right in the middle of it. Can you imagine if you're the next salesperson and you're in the middle of your presentation and a plant or a gift from Ralph Roberts gets delivered? It sure wrecks your day. What are you going to say to top that? The customer remembers me that much more.

CAREFUL WHERE YOU PARK

When I drive up to a customer's house, I'm always careful how I park my car. For one thing, my car has my name and my company logo emblazoned on it. I want the neighbors to be able to see it. I want the neighbors to be able to say to my potential customer, "Wow, I see Ralph Roberts is selling your home."

But I also take care to not block the customer's driveway. The customer may have a teenager who needs to leave for work, or someone else who needs to get in and out. The last thing you want is to have to get up in the middle of your presentation and go move a vehicle.

That's when you lose control of the situation.

While I'm parking or on the way to a presentation, I always clear my mind in those final moments. Salespeople shouldn't be making last-minute phone calls or fussing with other details. Your job is to sell, so focus on selling alone.

POSITIVE ATTITUDE

While you're clearing your mind, work on your positive attitude. Whether you're selling cosmetics at a counter or fighter planes to Saudi Arabia, you must know that you're going to make that sale. Even if things are going terribly bad for you in your life, you've got to tell yourself, "I'm going to make this sale today." I'm so convinced that I'm going to succeed that if a customer were to look out their window when I'm walking up to their door, they'd see me talking to myself, saying, "I'm going to make this sale! I'm going to make this sale!"

KNOCK, DON'T RING

Here's a tip for you salespeople who, like me, make most of your presentations at the customer's home. When you get to the front door, knock, never ring. You will lose that sale if you wake up the baby by ringing the doorbell. Customers with toddlers taking naps will appreciate your thoughtfulness.

Sometimes I may have to knock for several minutes before the homeowner hears me. Then she'll ask me why I didn't ring the bell. I'll tell her I didn't want to wake up any children who may be sleeping. The homeowner is almost always surprised and pleased with the trouble I've gone to.

THE MIRRORING TECHNIQUE

Whenever dealing with customers—whether in person, on the phone, or by mail—I use a technique called "mirroring." It means that I mirror whatever verbal style or body language they're showing me. If a customer is loud and brash, then I am, too. If the customer is timid and shy, then I'm also quiet. If a customer communicates by short written notes, then I'll write short notes back. I find this technique usually establishes a rapport from the beginning.

IT'S THE LITTLE THINGS THAT COUNT

Not long ago, I went on a sales call to a woman's house on a typical snowy, slushy, midwinter Michigan afternoon. I was about the fifth or sixth salesperson to visit this woman, hoping to get the listing to sell her home. As soon as I stepped through her front door, I noted that this was one of the cleanest homes that I had ever seen. The hardwood floors gleamed. The rug was pristine. So I immediately took my shoes off and whispered to my assistant to do the same. Well, the woman really appreciated it. The conversation went like this:

Seller: Wow, you are the only real estate people who took their shoes off.

R.R.: You've got to be kidding me! The other real estate people didn't take their shoes off?

Who do you think got that listing? Taking off our shoes may have been a small point, but people have to know that you care before they care about what you know.

Let's review for a moment. Your customer has barely answered the door, yet we've already mentioned several things that will help you make the sale. *These are details that almost none of your competition will think about.* A good salesperson sweats all the tiny details. You'll be way ahead of others in your field if you do, too.

Step Three: Get Them Responding to You

The salesperson can establish control at the beginning by asking for little things. Since I'm usually in my customer's home, I sometimes ask for a glass of water. Sometimes my pen will skip, and I'll ask for another writing instrument from the customer. By bringing me the water or pen, the customer gets used to responding in a positive way to my verbal cues.

THE HANDSHAKE

Always shake hands, whether with a man or a woman. Never overpowering, but firm and friendly. It does more than establish rapport. It helps to evaluate your client. If it's a couple, sometimes you can tell from their handshake who's really the decision-maker. You need to know that.

By the way, there are many other ways to spot the decision-maker. For example, I often drive potential homebuyers around in my van on a group tour of available sites. The person who sits in the passenger seat next to me is a decision-maker. If you're a retail salesperson and a couple walks in, you can tell the decision-maker by how they talk and when. It's a good thing to make your own study of this.

EYE CONTACT AND SEATING ARRANGEMENTS

You must make eye contact with your customers. If you don't, they may not trust you. Furthermore, you won't be able to read their reactions to your questions. You don't have to lock on them and get into a staring contest, but you do have to appear friendly, helpful, and open to their thoughts and suggestions.

To facilitate eye contact, I always try to arrange the seating so that I'm directly opposite my customers. If there's a husband and wife, I try to seat them at the kitchen table where the corner meets, so they're close together with me directly across from them. Often, a homeowner will try to get me to sit in the living room for our discussion, but I like to get to the kitchen table right away. The kitchen is where friends sit. If you're in the living room, that's business. You want to be more like friends with them. To do that, you have to get them into their comfort zone, both physically and mentally. It's easier to do that in the kitchen than anywhere else.

Suppose your sales calls take place in a restaurant during a business lunch. In that case, you ought to sit so that you can face the rest of the room, while the customer must sit with their back to the room, facing you alone. You don't want your customer distracted by watching other people or seeing a waiter drop a tray.

Some auto dealers that I know like to put their desk out in the middle of the showroom, but that's too distracting for me. I like to arrange the seating so that I've got my customer's undivided attention.

ICEBREAKERS

Since I do most of my sales calls in a customer's home, I can find numerous little tags to establish a connection. I've lived and worked in the same area of suburban Detroit for more than twenty years now. Many of my customers are referrals from relatives and friends who have worked with me before. So when I see a high school yearbook on a bookshelf in a customer's home, I usually know someone who went to school with my customer. Or I can ask them how their relative who worked with me in the past is enjoying their new home. All these little things help to establish me in their eyes as not just a salesman but as a human being, too.

COFFEE, TEA, OR SOFT DRINKS

Almost all of my customers are kind enough to offer me water, coffee, tea, a beer, whatever. I almost always accept something. It helps to break the ice. If the customer comes to your office, it may help to offer them something. To refuse a courteous offer of a soft drink may actually offend some customers.

Speaking of not offending customers, stay away from three minefields—sex, politics, and religion. There is no way you can win and many ways you can lose. If a customer brings up the topic, try to deflect it and get back to the question of the sale. Maybe like this:

> *Customer:* What'd you think about that presidential debate last night? Weren't those guys nuts?
>
> *Salesperson:* Yes, it was pretty wild, but mostly I've been so busy helping my customers I haven't had much time to focus on it.

DEMONSTRATING YOUR EXPERTISE

Without showing off, you will find many ways to demonstrate to your customer that you know your product. When I tour a home with a buyer or seller, I often open up the control panels of the furnace and hot water heaters, jotting down the pertinent technical data. Customers ask me why, and they're surprised and pleased when I explain how it helps me help them if I know everything about this house. I'm always looking for ways to stand out in the customer's mind.

That means doing more than other salespeople.

All salespeople need to make a thorough study of the product they sell. If we don't know our product inside and out, what good will we be to our customers?

Step Four: Guiding the Conversation

As I've said before, many prescripted formats that you try to follow may be doomed. We all, of course, have scripts; so do our customers. "May I help you?" and "I'm just looking" are examples of simple scripts. But don't get caught in the trap of relying *exclusively* on some prescripted approach to sales and service. As Nordstrom's Chris Younker says, "It's difficult to say what our recipe for good customer service is, because there isn't one. It has to be a way of life." But there are some ways of talking with customers that are more productive than others. Let's look at a few.

Here's a key rule: Ask questions that require some explanation from your customer, not a mere "yes" or "no" reply. The more the customer talks, the more you learn. The more you learn, the more you earn.

I want to be a great communicator, and a great communicator is one who listens. In my presentations, I probably do only 20 percent of the talking. The customers do the rest. The more the customer tells you, the more comfortable he or she gets in your presence. Remember, a good sales call is a chain of positive responses on the way to the final agreement.

One technique is to ask a lot of little questions that

you know will elicit a "yes." For example, if I'm trying to get the customer to choose me to list their house for sale, my chain of questions might go like this:

> "Is it okay if we put a 'For Sale' sign on your lawn?"

> "Is it okay if we include your home in our multiple listing service to get more inquiries?"

> "Is it okay to hold an open house?"

> "Is it okay if we use a lock box so other agents can get the key to show your home to buyers?"

> "Is it okay to put your home on a list given to transferees moving to this area from out of state?"

> "Is it okay to mail your neighbors to tell them we've put your home up for sale?"

By the time you get through asking ten or twenty easy "yes" questions like this, it's a lot more likely that you'll get the big "yes" at the end when you ask for the order to list the home.

Another technique is to feed back to the customer any question that they ask you. This brings out more of their thinking. For example, if a customer asks me what I think of a price of $100,000, I'll ask, "How do you feel about that price?" If the customer asks me what direction interest rates are going to go, I'll reply, "What does the changing interest rate mean to you?" Often I'll discover hidden fears or feelings this way.

This technique also helps me avoid giving a "wrong" answer. If a customer thinks that $100,000 is too low, I'd like to know that before I tell them it's too high.

Asking enough questions also lets you put your product in the best light. Sometimes a customer will call my office to ask about a four-bedroom house that has one of our "For Sale" signs on the lawn. The conversation might go like this:

"How many bedrooms does that house have?"

"How many bedrooms are you looking for?"

"Three."

"Perfect! This home has three bedrooms and a den."

Here's another example:

"Does that house have a big yard?"

"Are you looking for a big yard?"

"Actually, I'm looking for a small one I don't have to take care of."

"Perfect! This home has a very manageable yard."

So you have to learn how to ask questions that will bring out your customer's feelings. By the way, always ask how they "feel" about something, never how they "think" about it. You're after gut reactions, not vague thoughts.

Here's another technique. When you're trying to

understand what your customer is feeling, ask questions that elicit more than a one-word reply. I'll illustrate with a few examples from my own work. These are illustrations of some good and bad ways of asking the same questions:

Did you enjoy living in this house? (Bad. It requires just a yes/no answer).

What were some of the things you liked about this home? (Better. It requires a more detailed response.)

I see you told my assistant you think your home should be priced at $100,000. Is that right? (Bad. It can be answered with a one-word reply.)

What were some of the factors that made you choose that price range? (Much better. This question will elicit more information.)

How soon will you be ready to list your home for sale with a broker? (Bad. It doesn't require much beyond a simple response.)

What are the factors that go into your decision about when to list? (Good. It requires a more detailed answer that gets to the heart of the customer's thinking.)

It is crucial to know what your customer is thinking. The only way to learn is to keep asking questions until you get there.

PLAY THAT EMOTIONAL HIGH

I also try to tap into the natural emotional rush that most people feel when they see a home they want to buy. Say I've just shown a home to a husband and wife, and say the wife is oohing and aahing about the kitchen or the living room, but the husband is holding back. I'll jump in on the wife's side, and I'll be feeding back her enthusiasm with my own. "Yeah, wasn't that kitchen great!" or "You'll be able to do so much with that rec room!" I'll call up one of my assistants at my office on the car speaker phone and tell her that the couple liked the house. My assistant, who is coached to do this, will pick up on the enthusiasm and say, "Wow, we don't want to lose this one, but I know that a lot of other salespeople are showing it to other buyers." Then I'll say to my customers, "Do you want to go for it? Can you come up with the deposit right away?" And we'll work out as many details as we can right there in the car and finish them back in the office.

Step Five: Sell Like a Madman

I hate to lose. So if I'm representing buyers who are making an offer in competition with several other buyers, I always look for ways to set us apart.

A few years ago, I was representing a couple that really wanted to buy a certain house. The husband was a local city councilman, a lawyer, and a very authoritative guy. We were presenting our offer in person on Monday morning, so we spent part of the weekend trying to brainstorm ways to set ourselves and our offer apart from the others. First, I had my clients offer a bigger deposit than the other customers. Then I had the husband offer free legal help for six months to the sellers if they chose our offer. Finally, I had my clients write a letter to the sellers that said in effect: "Mr. and Mrs. Sellers, we love your home so much that we would be heartbroken if you don't sell it to us. But if you do sell it to somebody else, would you help us decorate whatever home we do buy?"

That letter worked so well that I often have clients write letters to the buyer or seller. If I'm representing a seller who has received a reasonable offer but wants to counter it, I'll ask them to write a letter to the buyer explaining why their offer needs to be countered. Sometimes the seller will say, "You know, it's no use squabbling over an extra $1,000 when we've already enjoyed the house. Let's just take the offer on the table." And so the deal is done.

Don't be afraid to go a little over the top in your sales presentation. I even leave little bottles labeled "Buyer and Seller Remorse Pills" with my customers. They're nothing but candy, but the bottle has my photo on it and the instructions to eat one pill whenever feeling remorseful over the transaction. Sometimes a customer will call me up laughing and tell me they ate the whole bottle. I guess it's not great if you're on Weight Watchers, but it sure helps to set you apart from every other salesperson out there.

QUESTIONS OF PRICE

Obviously, the price tag will be a major part of any sales conversation. In my business, where the price is always subject to negotiation, I try to use a range of prices when I work with my customers. Say a customer tells me his home ought to list for $80,000. I'll be able to show him that at $77,000 his home will sell within 30 days, but at $83,000 it will take 180 days. I can demonstrate this with detailed histories of other homes in the same neighborhood that sold. My industry keeps extensive records of all transactions, including how long a home remained on the market at each price level. When I share this data with my customers, they begin to appreciate whether it's worth waiting those extra months to get the higher price.

Homeowners who are selling their houses usually tell me what they think it's worth. It's my job to learn how they formed that opinion. Say a homeowner thinks we should list her home for $120,000. And suppose that seems high to me. By questioning her, I may learn that she's heard that a similar house down the street sold for that much. As an informed salesperson, I may know that the house down the street had a new addition that raised the value. Your goal is not to deflate your customer's expectations, but through persistent questioning, you can help them reach a more realistic assessment of the marketplace.

Sometimes when a homeowner insists that another salesperson has told them they can get a higher price than I suggest, I'll simply tell them to go with the other broker for a thirty-day trial. I know the home is not going to sell at that higher price. I'll tell them I'll call them in a few weeks and see how things are going. Often, they sign up with me after the trial period.

Suppose you're selling computers in a retail outlet. A customer may look over the latest laptop and comment, "Nice machine," then tell you he can get it cheaper at a discount house. Some questions you'll need to ask might include these:

> "Does your customer know what sort of warranty the other store offers?"

> "Does the other store include delivery and setup like your store does?"

> "Are the two machines really compatible? Minor differences in computers can translate into big price differentials."

> "Will your customer be able to get the face-to-face advice and counseling at that discount house that he finds in your store?"

And so forth. Almost every customer has some pre-fixed ideas about prices. By drawing out their thinking, you can demonstrate your own commitment to their best interests.

CHANGING "NO" TO "KNOW"

Along the way, you may—no, you will—hear the word "no." When you do, you cannot be discouraged. You must simply hear that "no" as "k-n-o-w," as in, "I don't know enough yet to say 'yes.'"

It's our job as salespeople to provide the customer with the information they need to change that "no" to a "yes."

ASKING FOR THE ORDER

A lot of salespeople ask me how I know when to ask for the order. Well, you should ask for the order continuously, but you may have to ask in a way that elicits that "yes" without scaring off the customer. I might ask a potential homebuyer, "Would sixty days possession work for you or would ninety days be better?" If you're selling new cars, you might ask, "How many people will be driving this car?" or "Will your teenagers be driving this car, too?" Such questions put the customer in the frame of mind that a sale will actually take place.

WHEN YOU HEAR "I WANT TO THINK IT OVER"

When people tell you "I want to think it over," you need to ask more questions. They don't really mean they want to think it over. That's just something they say so they don't have to come out with the real objection. In the automotive world, salespeople sometimes refer to these customers as "be-backs," i.e., those who promise to return at a later time but never do. When you hear "I want to think it over," you've got to keep asking questions until you learn what the real objection is. This process may require ten or twenty questions or more, but you've got to go through it.

Once you learn what the objection is, often you can turn it into a deal. Take the following example from my real estate practice:

> *R.R.:* So, Mr. and Mrs. Seller, would you sign the form now?
>
> *Sellers:* Well, we're not sure. We want to think it over.
>
> *R.R.:* What part of it do you need to think over?
>
> *Sellers:* Well, we thought we'd show all the forms to our attorney.
>
> *R.R.:* No problem. How about if I write on the form "subject to attorney's review and approval within forty-eight hours"? And then you can sign them that way.
>
> *Sellers:* But what if our attorney doesn't like this?
>
> *R.R.:* Then there's no deal, because I've added right here that it's subject to your attorney's review and approval.
>
> *Sellers:* Okay, in that case, we'll sign.

And they do. In most cases, they don't even bother going to their attorney. They sign right then and there. These customers just need reassurance that they're in control and that I have their best interests in mind.

Let's say you're a retail salesperson selling appliances in a large department store. You've been showing the latest model washing machine to a gentleman. It might go like this:

Salesperson: Well, can I write up the order now, sir?

Customer: I think I'd like to think this over a while first.

Salesperson: What part would you like to think about?

Customer: Actually, none of it, but I would like my wife to come here and see it first.

Salesperson: Okay, how about if I write up the order and you give me a check so we can lock in this sale price. I'll just put the check and the paperwork in the file and we won't put it through until your wife can come in and look this over. If she doesn't like it, we can tear up the check, but this way we'll have all the paperwork done and all she has to do is give her okay.

The customer in this case may not go along with it, but at least you're further along than you were before.

I've abbreviated these conversations, but you see the point. Keep asking questions until you find the real objection, then go to work on that. You have to be in control as a salesperson, but the customer has to be in control, too. They have to know that they're making the decision that's best for them. Making a major purchase, like a house or a car or a computer or a vacation, is stressful. Buyers really feel anxious during the transaction. It's our job as salespeople to make things as easy as possible for them.

If you're dealing with a couple and only one of them is reluctant, you can often handle that effectively with a little joshing. Recently, I was asking a husband and wife to let me list their home for sale. The wife was enthused and ready to sign the agreement. The husband was holding back. I couldn't get him to talk about his concerns no matter how many questions I asked. So finally, I said lightly, "Well, how about if we list just your wife's half of the house?" I'm not even sure where that came from. Anyway, they both looked at me like I was crazy. So I plowed ahead. "Sure, we'll sell her half of the house now, and when you're ready, we'll list your half later on." Well, pretty soon we were all laughing and breaking up. Then the husband unwound enough to talk about his concerns, and he eventually agreed to list his half of the house, too.

BE AGGRESSIVE BUT NOT PRESSURING

I know it's a fine line, but even after the sales order has been signed, if you sense the customer has serious reservations, you've got to back up and understand their concerns.

Here's one recent example. I was working with a

couple to list their house for sale. We went through everything, and they signed the forms to let me have the listing. But I noticed they looked uneasy. So I asked them what was wrong.

"We promised ourselves we wouldn't sign all these forms," they told me.

I said, "You knew I was coming over here to get the listing, didn't you?"

They said, "Yes, but we promised ourselves we wouldn't let you talk us into it."

I know I'm a powerful salesman, but they had felt pressured. So I told them: "Here, don't worry about it. Here's my entire file," and I handed them all the paperwork on their house, including the forms they had just signed. "What's your schedule tomorrow?" I asked them. "Sleep on it tonight, and if in the morning you still want me to list your home, drive the forms over to my office by 11:00 A.M." Well, they had the forms on my desk by 10:00 A.M. All they needed was the freedom to feel they were making the decision they wanted to make anyway.

Like those snow tires that Nordstrom's took back, you've got to always be thinking of your customers' best interests.

WHEN TO *STOP* SELLING

When the customer is ready to sign the order, quit selling. The selling's over. Whether it took an hour or three hours or any length of time, when they're ready to sign, shut up and take the order.

If you keep talking after that point, you are going to talk them out of the order that you've worked so hard for.

YOUR CHAPTER 8 CHECKLIST

✓ Am I keeping my customer's needs uppermost in mind?

✓ In any conflict between the customer's needs and my own financial benefit, do I side with the customer first?

✓ Have I developed a "silent salesman" kit of my promotional materials? Do I make sure all my customers have one?

✓ Do I confirm my appointments before I leave the office?

✓ Do I pay attention to all the little details when I meet the customer, such as where I park, where we sit, etc.?

✓ Do I do more listening than talking in my sales presentations?

✓ When I ask questions, do I ask in a way that elicits more than a one-word response?

✓ Do I enhance the positive atmosphere of a sales call through mirroring, feedback, and other techniques?

✓ Am I creative about questions of price to help a buyer or seller move toward a deal?

✓ When I hear "no," do I hear it as "k-n-o-w," as in my customer still needs more information?

✓ Do I always ask for the order?

✓ When a customer says they want to think it over, do I ask more questions to elicit their true objection?

✓ If a customer shows genuine remorse about a deal, do I give them a chance to reopen it?

✓ When the customer agrees to the transaction, do I know enough to stop selling at that point?

9

How I Found a Wife, Lost 100 Pounds, and Came to Believe in Miracles

ONCE YOU'VE REACHED THE PINNACLE OF SUCCESS, OTHER people think you've always been there. They see you winning awards, and they think that your every day and every moment has been an unbroken string of successful deals, victory celebrations, champagne bottles popping, and flashbulbs going off. Boy, can I tell you differently! I know from all the knocks I've taken just how hard it is to be a winner.

All salespeople get rejected, every day. It's part of our business. We hear many more "no's" than "yeses" in our daily work. Possessing the guts and the knowledge to get past the "no's" to the next "yes" is an essential part of our trade.

But adversity comes in many forms. Losing a sale is just one form—and hardly the most critical. We all face hardships in our personal lives. These hardships can hamper our professional development, too. Just at those times when we need to feel our best, when we're building our careers and going for that big sale, we may be burdened by troubles at home, financial problems, and personal drawbacks like being sick or overweight. Believe me, it's hard to feel up for your next sales call when you feel rotten about your personal life. I know. I've been there.

But we all can succeed in our personal lives, too. It's possible to have a spouse you love, a wonderful family, and your health and happiness. It's possible to have as much time as you need to give back to your community some of the good you've taken out of it. It's possible, in other words, to be a good human being as well as a good salesperson.

In this chapter, I'm going to tell you about some of the adversities that I've faced in my twenty-plus-year career. I hope these stories will help you realize that setbacks are part of everyday life, but that overcoming your troubles can become routine, too.

MY FORECLOSURE STORY

If there's one thing salespeople fear more than anything, it's financial failure. Maybe it's because we always feel we're just one commission check away from going under. Well, I can tell you from my own life that financial failure can be just one step in your learning process. I learned a lot from an early failure. I learned about how to do business to avoid such a failure again. And I learned about what's really important in my life—the respect and love of my family.

I was in my early twenties, a real eager beaver out to become a millionaire as quickly as possible. I was selling real estate by day, and I had bought a sports bar that I worked by night. I was buying investment property, and I was living in a home I had bought on a land contract. Under the terms of the land contract, I was obligated to make monthly payments plus a $5,000 balloon payment every quarter.

My finances were overextended, to say the least. I was making so many payments on so many things that I couldn't afford to cover monthly living expenses. I couldn't pay all my bills. My home insurance lapsed, and I couldn't afford to renew it. About that time, I got burglarized and lost about $15,000 worth of possessions for want of a $300 insurance policy. I remember that toward the end, I couldn't even afford a telephone in my home, so I slept with my window open so I could hear my car phone ring in my car parked outside. If the phone rang, I'd jump into my boots and run outside and answer it. I paid the electricity so that my water bed wouldn't freeze (this was the middle of a Michigan winter), but I had to cut back on heat, so I slept with lots of covers. My mother came over once and asked me why there was snow in the corner of my room. It was because I had to keep the window open so I could hear the car phone. Snow drifted in during the long, cold nights.

This was during that time in the seventies when interest rates kept climbing. Eventually, they hit 21 percent, and I crashed terribly. My payments on my investment properties just rose and rose. I was too ambitious to give up any of them, or sell my interest in the sports bar, or get a cheaper car. So I just kept on trying to juggle everything. I realized that I wouldn't be able to make the $5,000 quarterly balloon payment on my house payment. The holders of the land contract didn't care; they were hoping I'd default, because then they'd get the title back and have all the money I'd paid them so far.

I kept hoping that a miracle would happen. But it didn't, and the contract holders foreclosed. I hadn't told my family about my troubles, putting it off until five o'clock on the day I had to be out of the house. They pitched right in: They came over to my house and helped me load up all my furniture. They helped me find another place to live. They encouraged me to bide my time, that good things would come to me.

I guess that even without my parents I probably would have survived that episode, but having a family willing to share my load made it a lot easier. I learned some important lessons about getting overextended on the financial side. I've owned literally hundreds of properties since that cold day, and I've never lost another to foreclosure.

HOW THE WORST SALESPERSON I'VE EVER MET HELPED SAVE MY LIFE

I've always had a healthy appetite. In the eighth grade, I got cut from the football team because I wasn't big

enough. For a year, I lifted weights and drank milk-
shakes to get big enough, and I played first string on
both offense and defense in ninth grade. As I got older,
I kept eating all the junk food I could buy. My car was
a mess from all the Burger King wrappers. By the time
I was thirty, I weighed around 300 pounds. I was not
only the world's best salesman, I may have been the
biggest!

About three years ago, my wife and I were vacation-
ing up in Traverse City, a popular resort area in north-
ern Michigan. We were looking at sites for a possible
log home that we wanted to build overlooking Grand
Traverse Bay, a beautiful spot. We had to walk up
these steps from the water, and it was a hot day. I was
sweating and puffing, and I didn't feel too good. My
wife noticed it and asked me what was wrong. I said,
"I don't know, I don't feel real good, but I think I'll be
okay, maybe it's the steps." We had a real estate lady
with us, and I told her we'd call her tomorrow. We
went back down the steps and into town toward the
beach, because I thought I'd feel better if I had a
swim. Kathy told me that she hadn't packed any of
my bathing suits because they were all getting pretty
tight on me, so we stopped by this store in town to
buy one.

Well, whenever I see my tailor, he gives me a big
hello and tells me how good I look. The saleslady in
this shop, she did the opposite. She must have been
the world's worst salesperson, because she didn't do a
thing to put me at my ease. She grabbed this tape measure and slid it around my waist. She made a face and

announced to practically the entire store, "Fifty-two and a half." I said, "What! You must have it backward." But she insisted she was right. I grabbed that tape measure and turned it every which way, but I couldn't make the result turn out any different.

I wasn't real happy with that saleslady, but I bought three bathing suits and then turned to Kathy and said, "Kath, I need to go to the bookstore." I love to read, and I'm always buying all these things on how to be more successful, how to get more sales, how to plan for the future, how to be rich. So we went to this bookstore, and I bought about $300 worth of books and tapes on diet, exercise, and eating well. And if I have one secret of success that eludes others, it's that I actually put into practice the advice I read and listen to. Pretty soon, I realized I needed some help with my weight problem, so I enrolled in a course on diet and health at William Beaumont Hospital here in Detroit. I got some wonderful help from the doctors and dietitians and other specialists there.

I'm proud to tell you that I lost—and kept off—100 pounds. My diet is much better now, and I exercise regularly. It's made a tremendous difference in my looks, my health, my attitude, and my success. I'm selling even more homes today, and I'm doing it with less strain on my body and family. I'm sure that overcoming my weight problem helped me achieve this. I often think I owe a debt to that saleslady up in Traverse City. She may have been the world's worst salesperson, but she sure helped me.

MY TOUGHEST SALES SALE, OR HOW I FINALLY CONVINCED MY WIFE TO MARRY ME

My wife, Kathy, and I had met years before we started dating. She worked as a secretary in a real estate closing office, and I used to buy a dozen roses and hand them out to the young women in the office. That office had a policy that salespeople had to wait three days after a closing to get our commission checks. I don't like to wait, so I bought them all roses. Do you know, I never had to wait for checks? And Kathy says now that she remembers me as always being the number-one salesperson, but neither of us ever had any interest in each other romantically at that time.

Well, this was about the same time I lost my home to foreclosure. Eventually, I went to live in a room above the sports bar I owned. My brother and I owned the bar together, and we worked like crazy to make it succeed. I was selling real estate by day and tending bar at night. In our spare time, my brother and I would visit local softball fields and auto plants to promote our bar. We would cash paychecks for factory workers and deliver lunches to the Dodge plant across the street. We were packing in people after a while. It was wall-to-wall business for a couple of years. And one day in January 1984, several young women walked in after a bowling night and Kathy was among them.

Well, I took one look and knew that I was interested in her. I started to try to talk to her. She wasn't too interested at the time, but I was. I always had a dream.

I always knew I was going to be successful, even during the period when I lost my home. I knew I was going to make it. Les Brown says that when you fall down, if you can see up, you can get up. I always felt that at this time. But I didn't want someone to marry me for the wrong reasons. I didn't want someone to marry me because I sold a lot of real estate, because I owned a lot of rental houses, because I drove a Corvette, or any of that. I wanted her to love me and take care of me and raise our kids.

Well, Kathy had no interest in me at first. None. She would not give me her phone number, but I wouldn't take no for an answer, so I tried to get her phone number from one of her girlfriends. Her girlfriend wouldn't give me her home phone number, but she did give me Kathy's number at work. I called her and we talked a bit, not much. But I had found out from her girlfriend that one of Kathy's favorite places was this pancake house nearby, so the next time I called, I said, "I'm thinking about going over to the Pancake Pantry. Would you like to meet me there or should I pick you up?" I gave her two options, so it wasn't a "yes" or "no." So that was our first date.

I guess I was pretty mixed up about this time. I knew I wanted a wife and kids, but at the same time, I was afraid marriage would interfere with my sales career. So I was pretty conflicted sometimes about what to do. I was also dating other women at the same time I was seeing Kathy, and after a while, she got pretty tired of that. One time she was with me and this woman who I had just broken up with called me on my pager—that pager where you can hear them talking. Before I could turn it off, there were five seconds of just pure agony. I remember that after that, Kathy told me she never wanted to see me again.

Even so, that weekend was her sister's graduation, and I had told them I would bring the beer. So even though Kathy had told me she didn't want to see me again, I showed up at the graduation party with a keg of beer from my bar. I can remember taking the keg over to her mom and dad's house, setting it up, putting it on ice, hooking it up, and nobody talking to me. Nobody. Not her mom, not her dad.

Shortly after that, Kathy went on a vacation to Pennsylvania with her girlfriend. She toured the wine country and was gone, I think, ten days. A couple of days after she had left, I realized I hadn't talked to her in a few days and I knew that I was never going to get to talk to her again. I thought to myself, That's crazy. I've *got* to talk to her. I love her.

So I started calling people. I called her mom. I said, "Mrs. Paczkowski, I know you don't want to talk to me, I know I'm a bad person, I know that. But I have to tell Kathy something. I have to get her number, I have to tell her something." She told me she didn't have Kathy's number in Pennsylvania, although she probably did. So I started calling Kathy's girlfriends, and they were worse than Kathy's mom, refusing to talk to me at all. I tried one of their boyfriends, and I told him that he had to help me. Well, he found the name of a town in Pennsylvania where Kathy might be staying. So I started calling. This is when I realized I was a true salesman. It was like prospecting. I made over $300 in calls. I called all these people who might know where she was staying. I even called the state police.

Finally, I found the right motel room. I remember that Kathy's girlfriend answered the phone and said, "Kathy, it's for you." I could hear her saying, "For me? No one in the world knows I'm here." The girlfriend came back on and said, "Kathy Paczkowski from Michigan?" And I said, "Yes, she's there on vacation." So Kathy picked up the phone and I said, "Kathy, please don't hang up. I love you. I have to see you when you get home. We have to sit down and talk. Please give me that opportunity. Life is too short for me to miss this opportunity." I remember asking her when she'd be back. She told me, and I said, "Okay, we'll meet then." I remember meeting her again and talking to her and realizing that I wanted to spend the rest of my life with her.

Well, by the end of that year, we went over to her mom and dad and told them we were going to get married. I can remember her mom's jaw went all the way to the floor and popped up again. That was a long time ago, and today I have not only Kathy and our three beautiful kids, but great, great in-laws, too. Just a few years ago, for Christmas, my in-laws gave me a gift-wrapped Pennsylvania phone book for a present.

HOW BUILDING OUR FAMILY CONVINCED ME THAT MIRACLES REALLY DO HAPPEN

Kathy and I were married in 1985. We wanted a family badly, but it turned out that Kathy has something called endometriosis, which causes problems in conceiving a child. We wanted a baby so bad that Kathy had painful surgery several times following our wedding in an attempt to make conception possible. Still, the doctors told us that it was unlikely that she would ever have children naturally. Even though the odds were against us, we refused to give up. Finally, after months of hope and pain and worry, Kathy became pregnant. Nine months later, we were blessed with Kolleen. We were overjoyed with our good fortune. As I sat in the hospital room holding our tiny newborn baby, I knew everything had been worth it. All the sleepless nights spent wondering, all the physical and emotional anguish— the whole ordeal had been more than worth it. We now had an incredible gift, our first child.

But Kolleen was an only child, and we wanted her to have a sibling. Kathy and I decided to try again. Our doctor told us from the beginning that our chances were almost zero of having another child, but she said she would help us try as long as there was a chance— no matter how slim—that we would be successful. We figured that if we had endured the process once to add Kolleen to our family, we could do it again for the chance to give her a brother or a sister. We went through lots of tests. It seemed like Kathy was always at the hospital—sometimes several times in a single week. We tried different, special things while attempting to conceive. The stress of the experience played with our emotions. At the same time, we felt both hopeful and defeated, anxious but frustrated. All the while, the news from the doctors remained the same:

We could continue trying, but we probably wouldn't have another child naturally. We were getting discouraged. Kathy was getting tired of being poked and prodded. She was exhausted from the constant hospital visits and weary of the various drug therapies and invasive treatment she was enduring. Finally, after a few years of trying, the doctors encouraged us to stop. They said that Kathy would never be able to get pregnant and have children on her own again. We decided to finally listen to the doctors' advice. I realized the incredible strain I was putting on Kathy and did not want to see her in pain anymore.

Kathy and I were both mentally exhausted. Adding another child to the family had dominated all of our thoughts and discussions for years. We spent a few weeks talking about what to do next. Reluctantly, we agreed that the doctors must be right. After all, we had tried everything, to no avail. It was difficult to convince myself that we could not conceive another child, but the reality was that our family would only continue to grow if we found some other method. Once we accepted that, something incredible happened. A whole new world of options opened to us—we could adopt, be foster parents, or host exchange students. When we admitted that we had other options to explore, it was like we had been wearing blinders that were suddenly removed. For the first time in years, we saw everything clearly. Our batteries were recharged, and we were ready to reenter the fray.

You've probably noticed by now that goal-setting is something that I do on a regular basis. It was no different then. We had a list of objectives we were working toward achieving, and at the top of our list was having another child. If you learn nothing else from me, remember that you have to set goals for yourself and imagine they are real to make them happen. Sometimes it was difficult, but Kathy and I worked really hard at envisioning what our lives would be like after the new child joined our family. We even built our home with three bedrooms—one for Kathy and me, one for Kolleen, and one for the baby we knew we were going to find. *We knew it would happen.*

We began exploring adoption as the way to have our second child. But when you try to adopt, it becomes more difficult if you already have a child. Most adoptions are done for couples who have no children at all. Some days it seemed like we were just hitting one dead end after another. It would have been easy for us to just give up on having a second child. After all, we had a wonderful daughter. Yes, it would have been incredibly easy to just throw in the towel, but thankfully, we didn't do it. Our desire to have another child was a fire burning inside us that could not be extinguished.

For years, I had sold more houses than anyone else in America. I make things happen every single day. I run my company, I make decisions, I help people buy and sell houses. I finally decided that it was up to me to make this happen. I began telling everybody I knew that we wanted to adopt a baby. I told every person I met—every listing appointment, every buyer, every seller, every investor.

One day at a real estate closing, a lady sitting across the table from me was six months pregnant with her seventh child. She was not married. I started telling her how great it must be for her. I explained that my wife and I had been trying to have a second child for a long time, but the doctors said it wasn't possible. In fact, I said, we were now trying to adopt a child, but hadn't found one yet. I asked her if she had ever thought of putting any of her children up for adoption. Perhaps the new baby. She looked at me like I was crazy. "No, absolutely not," she replied in amazement. There was a man at the closing named Karl Strek who is a very good friend and advisor of mine. "It's amazing, Ralph," he chuckled, "you will ask anybody anything!" I knew there was almost no chance of adopting her baby, but we wanted one so bad, I was willing to ask just about anyone to help. I told Karl that I had blinders on until Kathy and I reached this goal. "You can't blame me for trying," I added.

A couple of months later, the most unbelievable thing happened. The woman from the closing called my office and asked me if I was serious about adopting a baby. I said I was extremely serious. She told us we could adopt the baby she was carrying. My heart raced as I listened. It seemed like a dream, but it was really happening. I didn't tell Kathy yet, because I was afraid of unnecessarily getting her hopes up again. But that night, I secretly rejoiced—our goal seemed close to becoming a reality.

Then the birth father brought the whole process to a halt. He would not allow the birth mom to give up the baby. Without his permission, the adoption could not happen. It was a crushing blow—it brought me as close as I ever got to giving up. But after several days of soul-searching, I knew that we had to continue following our dream. We would ride this emotional roller coaster until another person joined our family. In the end, this false alarm made me more determined than ever.

A few months later, I received a telephone call. I was at the office with Kolleen while Kathy was at aerobics. I was returning phone calls and doing paperwork. The call was about the birth father—he was ready to sign off! He would let us adopt his son! I thought about the most recent disappointment and tried not to get too excited, but I couldn't help it. As Kolleen and I rushed to the house to pick up the baby, I told myself over and over again that this time was for real.

When we got to the house, the birth mom was there, but the birth father was not. I took a deep breath and said I would not take the baby until I talked face-to-face with the birth father. The mom said she would go and pick him up and left Kolleen and me there to mind the new baby boy. He was wearing a white one-piece suit with a big blue sailboat on the front. His face, hands, and bare feet were filthy, and his diaper needed changing. As I held him, he stared up at me with those blue eyes—he was probably wondering who the heck this person was who was holding him. I realized that I was falling in love as I stroked his dirty strawberry-blond hair. I fought my emotions, trying not to get too attached to him too quickly, but it was already too late. I knew that if Kathy and I were disappointed again, I would be devastated. The room seemed to be getting hotter as I wondered what was taking the birth mom so long. How could she just leave Kolleen and me sitting there waiting? You can't imagine what I was feeling—we were so close to realizing our dream, but at the same time, in danger of being disappointed again. I was light-headed, and my heart was racing. The time passed so slowly; it seemed like an eternity. I began wondering if the birth mom would ever return.

I was startled when the phone rang. I looked around the room like someone else would answer it. Finally, Kolleen asked, "Aren't you going to get it?" I picked up the phone, and it was the birth mom. She had been in a car accident on the way there. I asked her if she was all right, but deep inside I selfishly worried that this development would somehow change her mind. I breathed a sigh of relief when she said she was fine and they were on their way back. As I hung up the phone, I wondered what else could happen to make us sit even longer. I got my answer a few minutes later when she called back again to let me know that they had a flat tire and would not be back. She put the birth father on the phone. My heart was in my throat and my mouth was dry as we began to talk. I knew I was making the most important sales call of my life: I had to sell the father on the idea of letting Kathy and me adopt this baby boy. The birth father was reluctant, then more cooperative, then hesitant again. I talked like I've never talked before. As the discussion progressed and I became more confident that this baby boy would be joining our family, a rush of adrenaline energized me. We ended the call agreeing that it was best that I take the baby home right away and we would work out the final details later. I couldn't believe it. I kissed and hugged the baby. I kissed and hugged Kolleen. We practically danced out the door as we left.

I was grinning like a fool as we drove home. As you probably know by know, I'm a little different from most people. I have a lot of enthusiasm. I grabbed the car phone and furiously dialed numbers of everyone I could think of. I had to share this with someone before I burst. I called home, trying to reach Kathy, but there was no answer. I tried calling her parents before remembering they were in Portugal—imagine their surprise when Kathy and I called them in Portugal that night to tell them about their new grandson! I dialed my own parents. Finally, someone was home. I tried to explain what was happening. They didn't believe me at first, but I was able to convince them. They headed to our house to help out. I telephoned all our relatives—my brother, Jeff, and his wife, Kathy; Kathy's brother, Mark, and his wife, Mary Ellen; Kathy's sister, Roxann, and her husband, John. I'm sure I dialed a bunch of other people, too. Since we had nothing ready at the house, most everyone scattered to stores to pick up stuff that we would need—diapers, formula, etc. I called home again; this time Kathy answered. I was so excited. I wanted to share the story with her, but I didn't know where to begin. The baby was crying, the radio was wailing, Kolleen was talking, and I happily said everything that popped into my mind. I was so overwhelmed with joy that I couldn't speak clearly. The other end of the line was silent. Kathy was astounded. She had just stepped out of the shower and was getting ready for a relaxing evening at home. She didn't know what to make of her crazy-sounding husband and the happy noises coming from his car. When I hung up, I still wasn't sure that she believed me.

I pulled into the driveway, opened the car door, picked up our new son—Kyle—and took him toward our home. Kathy met us at the door. She was wearing a blue sweat suit and her hair was still wet from the shower. She had never looked more beautiful. There was a light in her eyes—I knew she was going through the same emotional struggle I had. "Whose baby do you have?" she asked, arms defiantly stretched across the doorway. I said, "Kathy, this is your baby!" She stared at me in disbelief. Again she asked, "Whose baby do you have, Ralph?" Again, I smiled and said, "This is your baby." I knew she was afraid of more disappointment, and I knew there was only one way to overcome that fear. I stretched out my arms and held our son in front of her. "Take your baby, Kathy," I said softly.

Kathy took Kyle in her arms. The bond was instant. She stroked his hair and looked into his blue eyes. She began to sob as she kissed his forehead and held his tiny hand in her fingers. "He's so dirty!" she cried as her smile engulfed her face and the tears streamed down her cheeks.

■■■

A few years later, Kathy became pregnant with our daughter Kaleigh. Our doctors were astonished. But then, if you once begin to believe in miracles, you'll find they happen all the time.

10

Power Partnerships and Exit Strategies

MAYBE YOU'RE ALREADY AT A HIGH LEVEL IN YOUR CAREER. Maybe, with the help you get from this book, you'll get there in a few years. But I'm confident that at some point, you're going to look around and say, "Okay, I'm a success. What now?"

This chapter is for that day.

Let's say you're earning $100,000 a year. That's great, but will it let you retire at fifty? Can you pay for your kids' college *and* enjoy financial independence at that level? Maybe not. You'll probably want to generate more income—maybe a *lot* more—but you may feel that you're hitting the wall in terms of improved efficiency, even after putting into practice what you've learned in this book. What do you do then?

I believe—and I practice—a further step. I leverage

my abilities through the use of power partnerships and exit strategies. These are tools that you'll develop once you're already operating at a high level of success. When you get there and develop your own, you'll find them richly rewarding.

WHAT'S YOUR EXIT STRATEGY?

In most sales businesses, when you quit selling, you quit earning. In a few industries like insurance companies and stock brokerages, when you retire, the company will buy your book of business for a percentage of what it generated. Or some companies will pay residuals forever. But in my business and in many other areas of sales, we don't have that.

So a legitimate question for you is this: What kinds of exit strategies do I have in place? We all want to be able to retire with financial independence. (Whether we actually retire is another question. When I was thirty, I boasted that I would retire at thirty-five. Now I'm fortyish and I think I'll never retire. But I still want to be able to.)

This is the big question for salespeople as we enter the twenty-first century. How do I exit what I'm doing? How do I cash out of all that I've built up? How do I turn it into something that will take care of me and my family?

Here's another way to look at it. If I die or get disabled, what happens to my company? Since I just hit my forties, I'm starting to think about that. What would happen to my kids? What would happen to my family? I know now that I have to put something in place that will survive when I'm not there.

All this leads up to the topic of power partnerships and exit strategies. These are systems that you'll put in place that build on all the good work you've done already. To give you an idea of what I mean, let me tell you again about my mortgage company.

ALLAN'S INSIGHT

As I've said previously, I started my own mortgage company on the advice of my friend, Allan Domb, the condominium salesman in Philadelphia. Allan visited me recently. I was so impressed at how my new mortgage company was doing that I gushed that if I had to do things over, I might have gone into the mortgage business first instead of real estate. "No, Ralph, you don't get it," Allan patiently corrected me. My real estate, he explained, is the basis for everything else. I have networks of customers who buy homes or condos from me. For very little extra effort, I can also provide them a mortgage. This generates new income for me at little extra cost. But if I had started a mortgage company first, I would have had no customer base to work with.

When I started my mortgage company, I made a lot of mistakes. I hired good people to run it, but it still was a start-up operation for a while. We had a lot of kinks to work out. Recently, though, one of the national mortgage companies called me and suggested we form a partnership. They'll train my mortgage staff, handle all the administration stuff, virtually take all the headaches off my hands, but still operate from my office with my network of customers. And the payoff is that I'll make more money than I would have had I operated it on my own. This national firm can add enough value to the operation so that even with them taking a cut of the profits, I'll still make out better. Naturally, I jumped at this chance. It's already working out for me.

MINE YOUR BASE FOR NEW GOLD

Let's back up. You may be just starting. All this may sound like a lot more than you need. Okay, that's fine, I understand that. But for those of you who truly want to be superstars, I'm trying to give you a view of the landscape. Even if you go from 5 transactions a year to 500, at some point you'll feel like you have everything under control. And being the restless salesperson you are, you'll be looking for your next challenge. This is where you'll find it.

A key to power partnerships is the intelligent use of the customer base you've already developed. But it's got to be a good fit. An insurance salesman may offer his customers financial planning services. A stockbroker may be able to interest her customers in investment properties. Those are natural extensions of the original line of products or services, so it's a good fit.

A friend and partner of mine in another project once asked me to join him in selling herbal remedies. That seemed too far afield from selling houses, so I said "no." But it's a perfectly natural outgrowth for me to set up my mortgage company. That's an intelligent use of my customer network for an additional revenue source.

DEREGULATION IS THE KEY

Deregulation is the key to other businesses I'm getting into. There used to be one giant phone company, Ma Bell, and one gas or electric utility in each town. Now we have lots of phone companies, and pretty soon we'll have rival utility companies vying to sell us our gas and electricity. Most of them will be in business as resellers—that is, they'll buy big blocks of time or usage from the main utility, then resell it to customers at a savings. That's where we, as intelligent salespeople, can come in.

The profit margin in these reselling businesses stems from a simple fact. The big phone companies and other utilities make so much money that a reseller can give customers a price break *and* still make a profit. It's happening all over America. I'm involved with providing long-distance service right now with one of the newer phone companies. I have a customer network I can tap into, and each of my customers can make money in turn by selling the long-distance service to their own networks of family and friends. As with all my systems, it takes a little time and effort to set it up, but eventually the revenue just rolls in.

I'm already doing this with phone service. I fully expect to be part of a reselling plan for gas and electricity before long. It's a perfect add-on to my real estate business, because all my customers needs phone, gas, and electric service. Keep in mind that I'm not building or servicing the actual pipelines or switching equipment; all I'm doing is providing a new administrative service. I don't even have to set up the new service company; all I do is work my existing network of customers and acquaintances. If I can provide them the same service at a lower cost, why wouldn't they buy it? Some of my customers may be reluctant to switch, but I guarantee them that I'll switch them back at no cost to themselves if they're not satisfied. It's a win-win situation.

Any good salesperson can be part of similar sales efforts. You can find these opportunities by reading the financial pages, networking, and seeking out financial advice from successful people that you meet.

A FEW WORDS ABOUT NETWORK MARKETING

The preceding discussion gets me into the broader topic of network marketing. A network marketer is one who sells not just a product, but who also lines up other sales reps to sell the product. The initiating salesperson earns a piece of the profit for every sale that one of the downstream salespeople makes. A good network marketer can benefit from several levels of reps below him or her. Amway is one of the better known of the firms that distribute their products through independent reps working in this way.

A lot of traditional salespeople deride the notion of network marketing. I myself stayed away from it for twenty years. I thought it had nothing to teach me and too little to do with my core business.

Now I feel differently. I can see how a good network plan can fit with my established business. And I see how I can operate my network business on the side without taking an undue amount of time and energy away from my main field. I've found that it's easier for someone in my position—a top producer—to interest lower-ranking salespeople to sign up for my network than vice versa. That means I can get a network established fairly quickly without devoting too much time to it.

Some people criticize network marketing as a pyramid scheme. Tom Bagby likes to ask them, "You mean like General Motors?" If a pyramid scheme is one in which the people at the top make money based on what the people below them do, isn't that true of GM and virtually all other corporations? The only difference between GM and network marketing companies is that at network marketers everyone at every level *directly* benefits from the production of those below them.

Why shouldn't a salesperson who works hard get some reward? That's what the sales profession is all about anyway.

So for those of you already producing at a top level, I'd encourage you to take a look at network marketing. It may be a fruitful way to enhance your income. I'd caution you first to only consider those opportunities that are extensions of your core business, and second, don't try it until you're already operating at a high level and know others who are doing the same.

NEVER STOP LOOKING

Exit strategies come in many forms. The power partnerships I've discussed so far are one form. They can provide the revenue it takes to fund your dreams.

Allan Domb represents another type of exit strategy. Allan has calculated that to retire as he wants to, he'll need to have 200 investment properties—all fully paid for—generating income for him. He's working his way toward that goal. When he gets there, he'll retire—or at least he'll be able to.

I could probably retire right now, if I wanted to. I'd have to cash in everything and arrange things the right way. But I don't want to. I get too much fun out of working with my customers. I still get enormous satisfaction out of meeting new challenges, like my mortgage company or my long-distance network or writing this book.

I am developing new income streams and new ways to leverage my success. My speaking tours are part of that. As I said earlier, I now command up to $10,000 per day for a speaking engagement. I'm already thinking about what my *second* book will be about. I expect to be recording a series of motivational tapes soon.

All these things have been built on my foundation of a good sales career. I expect to be helping my customers buy and sell their homes for a long time. But I also expect my sales career to branch into new and exciting areas, some of which I haven't even thought of yet.

YOUR CHAPTER 10 CHECKLIST

✓ Have I ever done any serious retirement planning, complete with income and budget figures?

✓ What specifically do I need to do to be able to retire when I want?

✓ Am I producing at a high enough level in my main field to branch out into sidelines?

✓ Have I considered ways that my broader network of business associates can help me expand into new areas?

✓ Does my new sideline fit into my core business? Can I take up the new business without disrupting the old?

✓ Have I ever considered network marketing as a valid addition to my career?

11

You're Not Living If You're Not Giving

A FRIEND OF MINE, ART FETTIG, A GREAT MENTOR AND someone I reach out to a lot, told me recently that success and happiness are two separate things. He added, success and happiness *together* are two of the rarest commodities in the world. Our president was on TV last night, and although I don't agree with a lot of what he says, I totally agreed when he said you've got to do more than just send in your check. You've got to try to keep your family together, you've got to work for others. I think that's really important. I think I'm much more successful today because of that.

Now, I want *you* to succeed. I hope my book helps you make a lot of money. But even more, I hope it makes you realize what's truly important in life. You know, we all think possessions are so important. They really mean nothing. Helping others is important. For me, helping families buy homes is important. My family is important. When Kathy and I got married, we had four grandmas at our wedding. When my daughter, Kolleen, was born, she had four great-grandmothers. My Corvette doesn't mean anything. I've got a wonderful home, an unbelievable family, nieces and nephews around the country. When I can have the Roberts family Christmas Party over at my house, that means something.

WE ALL NEED A HELPING HAND NOW AND THEN

Don't fool yourself into thinking that by helping others and putting your family and customers first, you'll lose out on commissions. I believe the opposite is true.

Let me tell you a story that illustrates this.

Last week I was on my way to a closing. I was already running late. I'm driving along and it was icy. At a sharp bend in the road, I spotted a car in the ditch. The people were standing on the side of the road and they looked okay, but I still started to slow down to help. My closing secretary, who was with me, said, "What are you going to do? You're already late. Maybe we should just call the police." I said, "I've got to see if anybody needs help here." No one was hurt, but the people from the car didn't even speak English and needed a hand. Well, a neighbor came out with a chain, I put my truck into four-wheel drive, and we got that car out of the ditch and on its way. I was twenty-five minutes late for my closing, but we got them out.

Anyway, the man with the chain told me he had just moved into his house a year ago. And he said, "If I had known how many people would go into this ditch, I would never have bought this house." Perfect opportunity. I gave him my brochure. I said, "Listen, here's what I do." He said, "Wow, I've heard of you." I said, "If you get tired of people sliding into the ditch, let me know, and I'll find you a home that doesn't have a ditch in front of it."

He may never call, but it's just another example of how helping others without hoping for any reward for yourself often pays you back in unexpected ways.

THE PLATINUM RULE

I mentioned my friend, Art Fettig, a moment ago. Art has developed a wonderful concept called the Platinum Rule. To explain it and how it's affected my life, I'll tell you another story.

Some years ago, after getting involved with the conventions and associations, I started really building relationships with salespeople around the nation. One salesperson from Florida and I hit it off really well. He came up to shadow me not once but twice. Kathy and I invited him to stay at our house. We got a lot of work done during the day, then went out on Saturday night for dinner with a bunch of friends. We were celebrating I forget what, and we were drinking a fair amount of wine. A couple at the next table sent over two bottles of champagne. Pretty soon, it became apparent that everyone had had more than what one would have thought was their normal share of alcoholic beverages.

The next morning, there was church planned, but everyone was moving a little slow. We got up and sat down in the family room, drinking some orange juice, looking at the newspaper, just lying low.

My friend says to me, "Man, did we have fun last night or what?"

I said, "I think we had fun, but I think we got a little carried away."

"Ralph, how often do you do something like that?" he asked.

I said, "I can't remember the last time I did something like that, but maybe once a year we go out and drink more than a couple of drinks."

He said, "I do that every day."

"No way!"

"I do that every day. I drink every day," he said again. There wasn't much more said about it. I didn't really get into it at the time. I didn't realize what was going on with this new friend of mine.

That evening was like a normal Roberts family night. We watched a movie and ate popcorn. It was winter, so we drank hot tea and used afghans to keep us warm. The next day on the way to the airport, my friend said, "Man, that was really different last night, to sit around and watch a movie and eat popcorn—it was a lot of fun."

Time went by, and later, this person sent me a note: "Ralph, you and Kathy saved my life." I called and asked, "I saved your life?" He said, "Yep, I'm in AA meetings and everything is fine. I finally realized that I don't have to be high or drinking all the time to get through."

He sent me a gift, a little paperback book entitled *The Platinum Rule*, by Art Fettig. He told me what I had done was to practice the Platinum Rule. As he put it, "You helped me without knowing it or telling anyone."

MY FRIENDSHIP WITH ART

I immediately read the book and was really impressed. I called up the author, Art Fettig. We struck up a friendship that's lasted all these years. He is an incredibly smart man who has a wealth of knowledge and ideas to share. I try to spend as much time with him as our busy schedules will permit, because Art has so much to offer and teach and share.

You really should read *The Platinum Rule*. It just costs a few dollars, and you can order it by calling Art at 1-800-441-7676. *The Platinum Rule* is a little hard to explain, but the idea is powerfully simple. For example, let's say you loaned some money to an acquaintance and he told you he would pay you back. But he doesn't—or can't—pay you back. He gives you a date when he will pay you, but you see him after that date and he still hasn't paid you. You don't say anything, because you feel terrible. And he doesn't say anything to you, because he feels worse than you do, and you don't even realize it.

The Platinum Rule teaches that the next time that

happens, you just give that money to him. You tell him: "Here's how you repay me. You *never* try to repay me. How you can repay me is you help someone *else* someday." The next thing you tell him is: "Please don't ever bring this up again. Consider the matter closed, don't worry about it." After that you tell him: "Please don't *ever* tell anyone about this. This is our secret."

The results are fantastic. You feel great about helping someone, and the person you've helped feels great about you. Here is a relevant example: Let's say you helped a young family in a sales closing by giving them $200 out of your pocket to help them get through some unexpected closing costs. You tell them, "Don't ever repay me. Don't ever tell anyone about this. Someday you can help somebody else." And you make them promise not to tell anyone.

A wonderful thing happens. They won't tell anyone about what you did, but they will tell everybody how great you are. After doing several more similar good deeds, I called Art Fettig and said, "I'm telling people not to tell what I did, but they're telling everybody all kinds of good things about me anyway." He said, "That's the Platinum Rule. There's nothing you can do about it, you can tell them not to say anything to anyone, but they're going to. They're going to say great things about you for the rest of your life. And now they're going to do something nice for another person in need."

I am now in the process of opening a foundation with a friend called the Platinum Foundation. Its goal is to help people who need assistance—for example, if there's a newspaper article on a family or person who has run into bad luck, the foundation will send out a small check anonymously to help them out. It will be accompanied with the Platinum Rule.

The more you give, the more you receive. I see the ripples of good that the Platinum Rule sends out in all directions. I can attribute certain things in my life, like adopting our second child, to doing good things and something good happens.

The Platinum Rule is a powerful book with powerful ideas. I give it to my new employees, and I give it out at every sales call. Art Fettig has a goal of getting the book out to 1 million people. I know I am doing my part to help him with his goal, and he helps me with some of my goals.

DO WHAT'S RIGHT AND THE REWARDS WILL COME

So that's what I'd like you to take away from my book. Help others without thinking of your own good and *you* will be successful.

When you're on a sales call, you may be sitting there with somebody and you're probably thinking, "Wow, if I close this deal, I'll make a lot of money." But I truly believe that you've got to take the money out of your calculation. You've got to do what's very best for the customer.

I've had customers come to me and say, "I'm thinking of selling my home." They want me to represent them, which means I'd make a fast commission. But sometimes I have to say to them, "No, the market's not right at this time" or "You should probably just refinance now." And when the time is right for them, I'll call them. I may not make my commission immediately, but my customers know they can trust me, and that will pay me back in the long run.

So try to give people the very best advice. Sometimes, when you're struggling and really need a commission, it may be very hard to put your customers first. But by giving people the best advice, they're going to send more people to you. You might lose that sale right there that you probably could have manipulated and made happen, but it will come back to you a hundred times over by doing the right thing.

YOUR FINAL CHECKLIST

✓ Do I think like an entrepreneur instead of an employee?

✓ Have I considered hiring my first assistant—or my next assistant—to allow me more time to concentrate on what's really important?

✓ Do I embrace new technology or fear it? Have I gotten the most out of the technologies I am using?

✓ Am I smart enough not to let the inevitable "no" answers get to me during my prospecting?

✓ Do I believe in self-promotion as an important tool for any salesperson?

✓ Have I developed systems to make my job easier?

✓ Do I pay attention to all the little details during a sales call?

✓ Do I have emotional resources to overcome adversity? Do I rely on my family and friends for support? Do I make time for them when they need me?

✓ Have I thought about the possibilities of wider networking to enhance my overall success?

✓ Do I believe in—and practice—putting the customer's needs before mine?

Index